Penguin Critical Studies

Romeo and Juliet

Graham Holderness was born i[n] ...
schools. In 1965 he entered J[...]
English and stayed on to take a B.Phil. in nineteenth-century literature.
From 1970 to 1971 he worked as a Research Assistant at the Open
University, lectured in English at the University College of Swansea from
1971 to 1982 and for the next five years was Staff Tutor in Literature and
Drama at the Swansea Department of Adult Education. He is now Head
of Drama at Roehampton Institute, London.

His publications include *D. H. Lawrence: History, Ideology and Fiction*
(1982), *Shakespeare's History* (1985), *Wuthering Heights* (1985), *Women
in Love* (1986), *Hamlet* (1987), *The Taming of the Shrew* (1989) and a
Penguin critical study of *Richard II* (1989). He has also edited *The
Shakespeare Myth* (1988) and *The Politics of Theatre and Drama* (1991),
and is co-author of *Shakespeare: The Play of History* (1988) and
Shakespeare: Out of Court (1990). He is currently working on a book
concerned with the cultural production of narrative.

Penguin Critical Studies
Advisory Editor: Bryan Loughrey

William Shakespeare

Romeo and Juliet

Graham Holderness

Penguin Books

PENGUIN BOOKS

Published by the Penguin Group
Penguin Books Ltd, 27 Wrights Lane, London W8 5TZ, England
Viking Penguin, a division of Penguin Books USA Inc.
375 Hudson Street, New York, New York 10014, USA
Penguin Books Australia Ltd, Ringwood, Victoria, Australia
Penguin Books Canada Ltd, 2801 John Street, Markham, Ontario, Canada L3R 1B4
Penguin Books (NZ) Ltd, 182–190 Wairau Road, Auckland 10, New Zealand

Penguin Books Ltd, Registered Offices: Harmondsworth, Middlesex, England

First published 1990
10 9 8 7 6 5 4 3 2 1

Printed in England by Clays Ltd, St Ives plc
Filmset in 9/11 pt Times New Roman

Contents

Introduction

This critical study will consider Shakespeare's *Romeo and Juliet* as a book that can be read, as a text that can be interpreted and as a play that can be performed. These differing manifestations of *Romeo and Juliet* may all be regarded as aspects of the same work: a play-script written by Shakespeare some time in the 1590s; a performance-text that was popular in the Renaissance theatre and that has remained in the theatrical repertory ever since; and a readable text that is still widely appreciated, studied and enjoyed, not least within the framework of the contemporary English Literature syllabus.

We call all these cultural products 'Shakespeare's *Romeo and Juliet*'. Yet whichever of these forms we look at, we are likely to encounter not a solid ground of common responses to a uniform object but, on the contrary, great variety in readings, sharp divergences of interpretation in critical analysis and wide liberty of interpretation in theatrical production. This book is not so much an attempt to establish and demonstrate what *Romeo and Juliet* is as an effort to describe and analyse the range of things it is capable of becoming when activated by the imaginations of readers, motivated by the argument and debate of critics and re-constructed in performance by the interpretative strategies of stage directors, film producers and actors.

Yet we begin with a powerful conviction that Shakespeare's *Romeo and Juliet* is a simple, identifiable cultural artefact. We also feel at the same time that it is (paradoxically) complex enough to contain all this imaginative, critical and interpretative activity, some of which seems so varied and free-ranging as to throw the play's uniform identity into question. But, from a common-sense point of view, we assume the presence of a straightforward narrative and dramatic construction that remains always, in any of its manifestations, Shakespeare's *Romeo and Juliet*. After all, the play's basic story seems both simple, treating of common experience, and unconnected to specific circumstances of time and place and history.

What could be more fundamental and enduring than a story about young love, sudden and passionate and all-embracing, threatened and pushed towards its tragic destiny by a range of external forces working in unintentional but fatal conspiracy? What could be truer to our sense of the universality of experience than a narrative that shows these young

1

lovers locked in conflict with parents and peers, cherishing the uniqueness of their passion and trying unsuccessfully to integrate it into a hostile and authoritarian adult world? The basic story of the play, considered as something independent of Shakespeare's drama, seems almost archetypal in its symbolic centrality, almost mythical in its timeless romance and enduring relevance. The basic situation of two lovers kept apart by parental control and family conflict, inspired by their love to cross boundaries of social division in a symbolic union that entails tragic consequences, could be (and has been) adapted to fit many historical situations apart from the one used by Shakespeare. The Leonard Bernstein/Stephen Sondheim musical *West Side Story* started with Shakespeare, but the central action of the story was moved into a completely different cultural situation, where racial hostility between ethnic groups in New York replaces the family vendetta of Shakespeare's Renaissance Italy. Was that operation possible because *Romeo and Juliet* is an archetypal narrative of fundamental and permanent human experience?

We would perhaps expect a story of young love thwarted to appeal continually to young people themselves, by offering the dramatic representation of a familiar predicament with which it is easy for them to identify. Love is experienced in *Romeo and Juliet* as an immediate and absolute demand, with which there is no possibility of compromise; circumstances force that love underground into secrecy and concealment; the emotion itself seems incommunicable to other people, most of whom in turn (whether intentionally or not) treat the lovers and their relationship with indifference or hostility; and throughout the play we see both Romeo and Juliet subjected to impossible or unsympathetic parental demands, bullied by members of their own generation and unable to express their emotions freely except to one another. Of course, in reality adolescent passion is often constrained by parental authority or custodial morality: but even where it is not, young people in love are apt to project the internal difficulties of their relationship on to a looming, shadowy conspiracy of external threats and prohibitions. So, in terms of both the reality and the fantasy of experience, *Romeo and Juliet* seems a story calculated to appeal directly to young people and, by virtue of its crystallization of an unchanging human reality, to all other readers or audiences of Shakespeare.

If we accept that *Romeo and Juliet* deals with a common, if not universal, experience of love and enforced separation, exactly how universal is the particular chain of events dramatized in Shakespeare's theatrical narrative? We can approach this question by being more precise about the forces in the play that challenge the relationship of Romeo and

Juliet. Why are the young lovers unable simply to follow their inclinations and be together? There are in actuality two forces of separation, intimately connected with each other: family and feud. Romeo and Juliet cannot marry or even 'go out' together, because one is a Montague and the other a Capulet, and because they are young. Their family dependence (neither can marry openly without their parents' consent) means that they are subject to the authority of their parents, and therefore to family loyalties and enmities. This situation precipitates open conflicts – such as Juliet's resistance to the arranged marriage with Paris – between the adult heads of the family and the younger generation, which certainly seem like archetypally familiar domestic difficulties. But while we think of the basic conflict as one within the family, between generations, this particular story is set in a context where belonging to a family entails, whatever the misgivings or reservations of the individual, a duty of opposition to another family. It is on account of the long-standing feud between the houses of Capulet and Montague that Juliet's parents are assumed to be inevitably hostile to the idea of a 'mixed marriage'. We do not see Romeo involved in internal family conflicts in the same way as Juliet: his parents do not even appear between the first scene and the third act of the play, and Romeo is more preoccupied with the hostility of the Capulets than with the resistance of his parents. This may show nothing more than an inequality of freedom between men and women in this society: but Romeo certainly does not confide in his parents, and we can assume that, like the Capulet parents, they would feel a natural hostility towards a love that transgresses the dividing line between the families.

Are we still dealing, in this story of a love that grows in the no-man's-land between two families at war with one another, with a 'universal' experience? Clearly there are many circumstances in which relationships can be poisoned or destroyed by situations of racial hostility, ethnic enmity or class division. We could easily see in such contexts – the middle-class family disapproving of their daughter's working-class boyfriend, the Jewish family trying to forbid their son's marriage to a non-Jew – typical 'Romeo and Juliet' situations. More pointedly, circumstances of open and violent conflict between countries, races or political groups – between, say, a colonized nation and an imperialist power – could readily bring a simple heterosexual coupling into conflict with family and community loyalties. It would be a simple matter to set a version of *Romeo and Juliet* in Northern Ireland – Joan Lingard's novel *Across the Barricades* (London: Hamish Hamilton, 1972) does exactly that.

The pervasive presence throughout the world of violent conflict and

3

deep-rooted enmity ensures a plentiful supply of analogous situations, where a simple relationship of love may cut across other binding obligations. Furthermore, the coexistence within British society of different ethnic groups with varying attitudes towards matters of sex and marriage can put us in closer touch even with some of the more 'archaic' aspects of the Romeo and Juliet story: an Asian girl expected by her parents to comply with an arranged marriage would certainly find Juliet's situation understandable. But do these factors make this particular play an expression of universal experience?

If we look again at the two forces that operate within the play's narrative and dramatic structure to prise and keep the two lovers apart – family and feud – we begin to see that this quality of universality may be more apparent than real. In Shakespeare's play family and feud are linked and interdependent terms in the structural conflict. There is, we could say, a vertical dimension of conflict, which takes place between two generations within a single family, between old and young. But there is also an additional horizontal dimension, the conflict *between* families that is rooted in the Montague–Capulet feud. This horizontal cross-family conflict has to be linked up with the vertical internal family conflicts before the conditions of a 'Romeo and Juliet' story can be fully realized.

Within each of these two separate spheres of conflict, we can feel that we are confronted by an apparently universal quality of experience. When we see Juliet being forced by her parents to accept marriage to a man she does not love, we can feel confident that the conflict is taking place within that vertical dimension of internal family conflict, and that it is an experience by no means peculiar to Shakespeare's England or Renaissance Verona. If we regard the feud as a symbolic representation of social division, then that too can seem depressingly universal. There are always social groups divided against one another, with degrees of intensity varying from ingrained prejudice and mutual dislike to violent civil war. But the story of Romeo and Juliet can not coalesce as a narrative structure until *both* these dimensions of conflict (vertical and horizontal, inter-family and intra-family) are linked with one another into a single unified narrative and dramatic action.

At this point the structural pattern formed by the narrative starts to look more unique and specific and (though composed of universal-seeming elements) not universal in itself. We all, at one stage or another of our lives, can find ourselves in opposition to our parents: but not all our families are locked into a violent conflict with another family group. We could all think of examples of societies bitterly divided by factional conflict: but that conflict need not be reproduced within each group by a conflict between the generations – in fact the very opposite is often the case, when families are internally united by the very strife that divides them against others.

West Side Story is recognized as an adaptation of *Romeo and Juliet*. By the term adaptation we would normally understand a version of the story that does not simply reproduce Shakespeare's text and Shakespeare's words but develops the basic story into a more or less different treatment of similar themes: transferring the action to a different time and place; substituting a modern script or screenplay for the Elizabethan text; translating the play into a new form, such as the popular musical. An adaptation, we might say, is formed by composing variations on a theme. But the theme on which *West Side Story* plays variations is not precisely the story of *Romeo and Juliet* as I have just defined it. In *West Side Story*, the feud between rival New York street gangs is conducted entirely by young people. The leading figures on each side are young men: Bernardo, brother of Maria (Juliet), and the equivalent of Tybalt in Shakespeare's play, heads the gang of Puerto Rican 'Sharks'; while Riff (who, like Mercutio in Shakespeare's play, is killed in a brawl as a consequence of intervention by Tony/Romeo) leads the white gang of 'Jets'. The respective parents of Tony and Maria are effectively excluded from the musical play. The lovers refer to them, but they never appear, except when as an off-stage voice Maria's mother calls her indoors during the musical's equivalent of the 'balcony scene'.

The structural pattern in *West Side Story* contains two generations, but they are not evenly divided, whites against Puerto Ricans, as Capulet and Montague are in Shakespeare's play. The conflict is between groups of young people who face one another across a bitter divide of racial hostility. The adult characters in the musical all stand outside the gang warfare and attempt to stop it. Doc (Tony's employer, and the equivalent of Friar Laurence) tries to reason with the gangs; the policemen Officer Krupke and Lieutenant Schrank try to stop their fighting by a mixture of persuasion and force; a well-meaning but hapless youth-club leader (comically named Glad Hand) tries ineffectually to unite the gangs at a dance (Shakespeare's Capulet ball). The role of Juliet's Nurse, who, of course, tended Juliet as a baby, is fulfilled by Anita, Bernardo's girlfriend, who seems not much older than Maria herself.

Now although this pattern has its basis in *Romeo and Juliet* (so that certain figures, such as Friar Laurence and Tybalt, can be more or less accurately reproduced), it does not imitate the play's narrative and dramatic structure, but produces another, different one, concerned with teenage violence rather than an old-established feud between two rival families. The musical, which dates from the 1950s (the film version was released in 1961), inflects the action of the play towards contemporary social problems (racial prejudice, street violence, youthful rebellion against authority) in a way that seems to confirm Shakespeare's story as one of universal significance. Yet in fact only one element of Shakespeare's structure has been employed, so that the story falls here into a quite different narrative and dramatic pattern.

Ultimately the question I am addressing resolves into a simple choice of alternative explanations. Does Shakespeare's *Romeo and Juliet* contain, within its narrative and dramatic structure, a story of universal application and consistent meaning, which can be mobilized to say virtually the same thing in many different cultural and historical situations? Or does the apparent timelessness of the story derive from continual reworkings of the basic idea to fit different cultural and historical situations, with each version being more a production of its own time and place than a restatement of Shakespeare's text?

This is not of course a question that can be simply answered: and since the issue at stake is probably the most contentious problem in contemporary literary studies, we would not expect to resolve it in the discussion of one play. Overall this study will provide more evidence for the second view than for the first. In the following pages we will be looking at the variations between different versions and retellings of the 'Romeo and Juliet' story, both before and after Shakespeare's play; at the differences between the performances and printed texts in which the play appeared during the Renaissance period; at the divergences between different critical interpretations; and at the variety of different theatrical adaptations of the play in more recent cultural history. Before taking this exploration further we will need to undertake some consideration of the play's structure, the particular narrative shape in which the story of Romeo and Juliet is actually dramatized, enacted and conveyed.

1. Story and Structure

By structure I mean two things: first, the way the story is constructed in terms of the narrative organization of its action, the dramatic ordering and linking of its events, the overall shape of the play. Secondly, structure can relate to the significance that the play's events, when so ordered, seem to contain or imply; so we talk of a particular 'structure of meaning', or 'significant structure', referring not only to the shape of the story but also to the way it presents and comments on its own shape, the kind of meaning its form seems to require.

Now, although we may try to describe the basic structure as objectively as possible, it is in practice very difficult to separate description from evaluation and interpretation, since the shape given to the story in a particular version contributes substantially to the range of possible ways in which it can be interpreted. The summary of the play's action that occupies the following pages is not therefore a skeletal synopsis of external events ('Romeo sees Juliet, falls in love') but an analytical summary of the play's dramatic and narrative structure, pointing out devices such as parallelism and repetition, drawing attention to particularly complex or significant juxtapositions, highlighting not just the way things are organized in the play, but the sort of meaningful pattern formed when those things are placed into that particular narrative and dramatic structure.

Act I

SCENE 1

The opening scene introduces the feud, the general theme of love and one of the two lovers, Romeo. We witness two groups of servants, attached respectively to the two rival houses of Capulet and Montague, looking for trouble and starting a fight. Benvolio, a character who consistently tries to remain neutral in the conflict (his name means 'well-wisher') but whose kinship ties are with the Montagues, tries to stop the fight. He is, however, clearly identified as a Montague by Juliet's cousin Tybalt, who engages him in swordplay. The heads of the two houses, Montague, Capulet and their wives, join the fray themselves. The riot that Escalus, the Prince of Verona, intervenes to stop thus involves both masters and servants, both older and younger generations, both men and women. The society of Verona is split directly in two along family lines, with the Prince standing above the conflict, representing a civil authority that transcends the violent partisan loyalties active in and between the two houses.

So far there is much to do with hate, but nothing about love. Lady Montague, discussing the brawl with her husband and Benvolio, mentions her son Romeo almost by way of changing the subject:

> O where is Romeo? Saw you him today?
> Right glad I am he was not at this fray.
> (I.1.116–17)

In accounting for Romeo's absence Benvolio describes the conventional behaviour of a young man in love, retreating from society wrapped up in his own self-indulgent melancholy. When Romeo appears, he himself confirms this impression, speaking a language of love that is self-consciously decorative and poetic. There is no mention of the identity of the girl – it is as if Romeo hardly needs a partner, so much is he enjoying his unrequited affection – though it becomes clear in the next scene (I.2.82) that Benvolio knows the object of Romeo's passion to be one Rosaline, a niece of Capulet (see I.2.68). Everyone else seems to know this too, except perhaps Romeo's parents: Mercutio and Friar Laurence – a friend and a father confessor – both mention Romeo is still in love with Rosaline (see II.1.17 and II.3.40). Curiously, nobody in possession of this knowledge thinks to point out that as Rosaline is Capulet's niece, a relationship with Montague's son would transgress the boundaries of family discrimination in the same way, if not to precisely the same degree, as does Romeo's passion for Capulet's daughter Juliet. It is as if nobody, Romeo included, expects this infatuation ever to become real enough to cause any trouble or do any damage.

Some of the relationships between family hatred and romantic love are also articulated here at the beginning of the play. The existence of the feud seems to have no bearing on Romeo's love for Rosaline: as a passion of introversion, his desire withdraws him from that particular area of human society into solitude and fantasy. Surveying the remains of the brawl, Romeo declares them irrelevant, or useful only to provide metaphors for the turbulent ecstasies and violent intensities of love. Certain chauvinistic attitudes to women thus coexist with the feud: the aggression of the servants ('women, being the weaker vessels, are ever thrust to the wall', I.1.14–15), and the refined romantic passion that Romeo harbours for Rosaline.

At the same time, it is clear from the conversation between Romeo and Benvolio, towards the end of this scene and in the next, that Romeo himself has little difficulty integrating this particular emotion with the normal conventions of Veronese society. His desire for Rosaline does not prevent Romeo from playing a full role in ordinary social intercourse; even the elaborate rituals of social withdrawal described earlier by Benvolio are perhaps only to be expected from a young man in love.

SCENE 2

Scene 2 introduces us to the head of the Capulet family, Juliet's father, discussing with Paris the question of his daughter's marriage. Here Capulet seems determined to put Paris off and to defer Juliet's marriage until she is older. The fact that the two men, father and suitor, are discussing a girl's marriage without her knowledge gives a fair idea of the marriage system operating in Verona. On the other hand, Capulet's attitude seems, within this context, to be very fair: he gives Paris permission to woo her, but insists that Juliet herself should choose her marriage partner.

> But woo her, gentle Paris, get her heart.
> My will to her consent is but a part,
> And, she agreed, within her scope of choice
> Lies my consent and fair according voice.
> (I.2.16–19)

Capulet's consent to a marriage for Juliet will be withheld until his daughter has agreed: it is up to the young man himself to persuade her. Meanwhile, the father makes it clear that he would rather Juliet did not marry too young. He invites Paris to 'an old accustomed feast' at the Capulet house that evening, suggesting that there will be plenty of other girls there for him to admire (in the event, Paris does not appear there). Capulet then gives an invitation list to a servant (in the Elizabethan texts he is called 'Clown', the term usually given to a basically comic minor role: he is not actually a professional 'jester').

The Clown evidently cannot read, and is therefore unable to decipher the invitation list: he needs help from someone with education ('I must to the learned. In good time!', I.2.43–4). His assistance arrives in the form of Benvolio and Romeo, who reads the invitation list for the servant, and in this way learns about the feast, and about the fact that his beloved, Rosaline, is invited. Benvolio suggests that if Romeo were to go there and compare his love with other ladies, he would be disillusioned with her and cured of his passion. In other words, Benvolio gives to Romeo exactly the same advice Capulet gave to Paris at the beginning of this scene: and in the event Romeo does exactly what Benvolio advises him to do. Ironically, neither Rosaline nor Paris actually appears at the feast: at least they are not named in the stage directions as being among the guests present. Rosaline does not figure in the *Dramatis Personae* (cast list) at all, so she remains, as far as the audience is concerned, a figment of Romeo's imagination, and is not there to witness Romeo's remarkable conversion from one love to another. It is also perhaps fortunate that Paris is not present to watch his would-be fiancée falling in love with another man.

SCENE 3

Juliet is now presented in the ordinary domestic context of a young unmarried girl, flanked by mother and Nurse. For a while the Nurse's comic rambling keeps Capulet's wife from getting to the point, which again concerns marriage. Juliet's mother seems much more enthusiastic about the prospect of the marriage to Paris than did her father: the mother sees no barrier of age, and is fulsome in praise of the suitor. Yet another decisive encounter is planned to take place at the Capulet feast: Juliet is to see Paris and, according to her mother's wishes, acknowledge him as an ideal marriage partner. Clearly a dramatic and narrative pattern has formed here, whereby the Capulet feast is anticipated by a range of characters as a site of potential emotional conversion: according to Capulet, Paris is to change his mind about Juliet; Benvolio hopes Romeo will become disillusioned with Rosaline; and Juliet's mother plans for her daughter to fall in love with Paris. All this concentrated focus on the feast induces in the spectator the expectation that it will prove an exciting and decisive dramatic occasion.

But, in the event, all the specific expectations of the characters go amiss. Paris is not there to compare Juliet to other ladies, so his intentions are not altered; Romeo is certainly cured of his love for Rosaline by meeting Juliet, but only by falling much more hopelessly in love with another girl, and not at all in the way Benvolio intended; and at the feast Juliet falls in love with what she sees, but not in line with her mother's pre-arranged 'blind date' with Paris, since it is not in his countenance, but in the face of Romeo, that she finds 'delight writ there with beauty's pen' (I.3.84).

SCENE 4

This scene sees the young Montague men, disguised in masks to conceal their family identity, discussing strategies for gate-crashing the Capulet feast. Romeo persists in his pose as the 'empiercèd' lover, unable to participate fully in his companions' carefree enjoyment, though again the generally light and comic tone of these witty exchanges indicates no deep or very serious wound.

The most prominent voice in this scene is that of a character here newly introduced, Mercutio. Mercutio stands apart from the other young gallants, both in his kinship ties – he is not a relative of the Montagues but, like Paris, a kinsman of the Prince – and in his boisterous and unpredictable energy. His name appears on the invitation list as a guest at the Capulet party, yet he prefers to sneak into the feast disguised, in the company of the Capulets' enemies. Mercutio performs a number of different roles in the course of the play: he is a mocking and satirical observer of folly, a cynical commentator on human illusions, a parodist, a satirist and a deflator of illusions. At the same time he is very much the life and soul of the party, striving wherever he goes to provoke and generate an atmosphere of carnival. In this scene he mocks Romeo's pose of the wounded lover in such a way as to draw Romeo out into the high-spirited wit combats that constitute an important leisure activity for these young gentlemen-about-town.

The morally corrective and socially therapeutic role of the satirist perhaps suggests a man more in control of himself than those around him, capable of observing from a stable emotional and moral basis the foibles and deviations of others. Mercutio is, however, far from this model of the ironic spectator. He is a man full of restless, irritable energies, craving excitement and the perpetual motion of wit, pleasure and incessant activity. Though not a kinsman of the Montagues, he is the one character to be killed in the street fighting of the Montague–Capulet feud, stabbed to death by Juliet's cousin Tybalt. Several of the roles Mercutio performs are focused in this scene in his famous speech about 'Queen Mab', the queen of the fairies. This remarkable rhetorical performance, which celebrates and investigates the powers of imagination, fantasy, narrative and dramatic reality and illusion, seems to me not just an occasional piece, a virtuoso solo aria, but a key philosophical statement illuminating the whole world of the play. I will therefore discuss it at greater length and in more detail when dealing with the play's theatrical language (see below, Chapter Three, pp. 37–8).

SCENE 5

In the Capulet house, Romeo observes Juliet dancing, and immediately speaks of love for her. The shock of this sudden emotion clearly puts him momentarily off guard: Tybalt recognizes him, and is restrained from attacking him only by the authority of his uncle, Capulet. This moment indicates that the inter-family feud is a rather more complex affair than we have perhaps hitherto supposed. While the young man Tybalt responds to Romeo's presence with immediate vindictive anger and ready violence, the head of the family forcibly pacifies his nephew and insists that the young Montague be left alone.

> Content thee, gentle coz, let him alone.
> 'A bears him like a portly gentleman.
> And, to say truth, Verona brags of him
> To be a virtuous and well-governed youth.
> I would not for the wealth of all this town
> Here in my house do him disparagement.
>
> (I.5.65–70)

Perhaps Capulet is still smarting under the Prince's recent rebuke, and is anxious to avoid similar trouble; or his generous admiration for Romeo may be genuine. Either way, there is a marked difference here between the older and the younger generation of Capulets in terms of their observation of the vendetta. The young hot-head confronts and opposes the elderly diplomat, at the same time as Romeo and Juliet unite in an emotional intimacy that dispenses with the family enmity altogether.

Romeo and Juliet meet in the dance, and he makes lightly veiled protestations of love, which she does not reject. The Nurse then calls her away, and Romeo learns from the Nurse of Juliet's identity. As he departs, Juliet asks of the Nurse the same question, and acquires from her the same information – that each has fallen in love with the child of their fathers' principal enemy.

Act II

SCENE 1

The basis of the action of the play has now been established, and Act I ends with what may seem a rather superfluous summary by the Chorus of 'the story so far'. We will examine later the use in the play of this and other narrative devices, 'pauses' employed to hold up the action, to re-tell an event already witnessed or to go over the particulars of an event in more leisurely detail than the main narrative sequence permits (see below, Chapter Three, pp. 35–6)

SCENE 2

Romeo enters, evidently seeking Juliet, pursued by his fellow revellers. He hides from them, and makes his way over the wall into Capulet's orchard. Juliet appearing at her chamber window, the lovers exchange confessions and vows of love (the staging of the action here will be addressed in an extended discussion of the famous 'balcony scene', Chapter Six, pp. 72–6).

SCENE 3

This scene introduces Friar Laurence, who as the father-confessor of both Romeo and Juliet becomes the confidant, adviser and helper of both. The Friar is a significant presence in the play both functionally (he is responsible for organizing much of the plot) and symbolically (since, like the Prince, he stands outside the divided polity of Verona, belonging to no family but to a Church that incorporates and transcends both). When Romeo admits to having been out all night, the Friar jumps to the conclusion that he has slept with Rosaline: evidently Romeo has been confessing his love to his spiritual adviser. Reassuring Friar Laurence, Romeo speaks of his love for Juliet in a language as complex and metaphysical as the Friar's preceding speech about the contradictory qualities of nature:

> I have been feasting with mine enemy,
> Where on a sudden one hath wounded me
> That's by me wounded. Both our remedies
> Within thy help and holy physic lies.
>
> (II.3.45–8)

After some routine moral exhortation of Romeo, Friar Laurence indicates a willingness to help, founded on a conviction that this emotional alliance may be used to bring the warring families of Capulet and Montague together:

> For this alliance may so happy prove
> To turn your households' rancour to pure love.
>
> (II.3.87–8)

SCENE 4

This scene returns to Romeo's companions of the previous night, Benvolio and Mercutio, who are still searching for him. Like Friar Laurence, they of course know nothing of Romeo's meeting with Juliet, and assume that he must have slept with Rosaline. The conversation naturally turns therefore, when Romeo appears, on a series of obscene and bawdy witticisms, in which Mercutio conveys cynical and salacious views on women and sex. Since the scene with Friar Laurence, in which Romeo expresses extremely pure and honourable intentions, precedes this meeting with the other gallants, there is a strong sense of contrast between the love he bears for Juliet and the kind of sexual experience alluded to by Mercutio.

Here Romeo appears quite the opposite of the melancholy, withdrawn figure of his earlier pose: he engages fully with Mercutio's pleasantry, and beats him in a combat of wits. Where Romeo's love for Rosaline apparently drew him, at least to some extent, away from society, his love for Juliet returns him to it. In Mercutio's opinion, this represents nothing less than Romeo's recovery of his own lost self:

> Now art thou sociable. Now art thou Romeo.
> (II.4.87)

Into this atmosphere of jesting and mockery, of suggestive allusions and dirty jokes, comes Juliet's Nurse with a message for Romeo. Again there is a strong sense of contrast, since the relationship the Nurse is helping to cement is a secret marriage, while Mercutio assumes that she is a bawd (pimp) luring Romeo to a sexual assignation. The Nurse here purports to be injured by Mercutio's mockery, though her own attitudes towards love and sex are nothing if not robust and broadminded.

SCENE 5

Juliet waits impatiently for the Nurse's return. When the latter appears, she deliberately keeps Juliet waiting for the news she longs to hear: that Romeo will meet and marry her at Friar Laurence's cell. The Nurse's language synthesizes the moral purity of Romeo's romantic discourse with the bawdy *double entendre* of Mercutio's sexual slang:

> I must another way,
> To fetch a ladder, by the which your love
> Must climb a bird's nest soon when it is dark.
> (II.5.72-4)

Literally this alludes to the practical means by which Romeo will enter Juliet's bedroom; figuratively 'climbing a bird's nest' (i.e. penetrating a girl's pubic hair) was a common piece of sexual innuendo.

SCENE 6

In this short scene the secret marriage takes place. There is an emphasis on the eagerness of the lovers to consummate their wedding – the stage direction signals that '*Enter Juliet somewhat fast. She embraces Romeo.*' The Friar issues some moral warnings against excessive passion – 'these violent delights have violent ends' (II.6.9) – but doesn't seriously expect them to be heeded. As far as he is concerned, their sexual passion is of such an intensity that the sooner they are married, the better.

Act III

SCENE 1

In a typically sharp juxtaposition, the wedding scene is followed by a return to the Montague–Capulet feud. In this scene the quarrel becomes genuinely serious, since it involves the death of Mercutio at the hands of Tybalt, Juliet's cousin, and the subsequent killing of Tybalt by Romeo. Despite his uncle's rebuke, Tybalt has decided to regard Romeo's presence at the Capulet feast as a personal injury, and seeks him out with a challenge. The initial conflict is not, however, between those two, but between Tybalt and Mercutio. The former is motivated by a controlled and determined vindictiveness; the latter (who, remember, is not a Montague) by restlessness and boredom. It is entirely possible, as some productions seek to suggest, that the fight with Tybalt is for Mercutio merely a game, which turns deadly serious only when Romeo steps in and tries to stop it.

Romeo's reaction to Tybalt's insult shows that he is trying to realize Friar Laurence's aspiration that a union of marriage between the Capulet and Montague children would lead to a union of the families themselves:

> ROMEO
> I do protest I never injured thee,
> But love thee better than thou canst devise . . .
> (III.1.67–8)

Whether Tybalt would have accepted this truce if Romeo could have revealed its basis, is an open question. Mercutio sees Romeo's backing down from the challenge as cowardice, a 'dishonourable, vile submission' (III.1.72), and he himself provokes Tybalt into a fight. Certainly it is Romeo's intervention, made with the best possible motives, that causes Mercutio's (possibly accidental) death. The Friar's plans, and all the hopes attaching to the secret marriage, are starting to go badly wrong.

Mercutio's death provokes Romeo to oblivious fury, and when Tybalt returns, the newly wedded Montague kills the Capulet who, unawares, has become his own cousin-by-marriage. The Prince arrives at the scene of the affray and, particularly angered by the death of his own kinsman Mercutio, sentences Romeo to exile from Verona.

SCENE 2

This scene parallels II.5, in which Juliet waited impatiently for the Nurse to bring news from Romeo. Here she again waits in impatient longing, this time for the physical consummation of her marriage. When the Nurse finally appears, Juliet again has considerable trouble dragging the news out of her. But the exactness of the parallel serves only to bring home how much has changed in these few short hours. In the earlier scene, Juliet had to suffer the trials of her own impatience and the Nurse's perversity, but was rewarded with the news of Romeo's promise of marriage. Here her aroused anticipation of first-night passion is thwarted by news of violence and bloodshed, and this time the Nurse's procrastination is due not to a practical joke, but to the serious and deadly nature of her knowledge.

The Nurse's inability to declare her message plainly forces Juliet through a succession of violent emotional reactions, as she imagines first that Romeo is dead, then that both he and Tybalt have been slain, then that Romeo's killing of Tybalt was a villainous act of treachery. Finally she comes to rest on a strenuous defence of her husband's character, on the basis of which she is able to reconstruct for herself an accurate picture of what actually happened. As she realizes the implications of Romeo's exile, she enters on a series of conceits around the word 'banishment', which will be echoed by Romeo in the next scene. Towards the end of this scene Juliet begins to link the vocabularies of love and death in a morbid though glamorous poetry that will rarely be absent from the rest of the play. The Nurse promises to find Romeo and bring him to her.

SCENE 3

Juxtaposed against Juliet's affliction we find a scene depicting Romeo in a precisely parallel plight – as the Nurse says, 'Just in her case' (III.3.86). Here the messenger and confidant is the Friar, who informs Romeo of the Prince's sentence. To Romeo the doom of separation from his love seems more terrible, as it does to Juliet, than the prospect of death itself: so he too elaborates on the power of the word 'banishment'. The Friar's well-meaning efforts to reason Romeo out of his despair through the teachings of religion and philosophy are to no avail.

The arrival of the Nurse only intensifies Romeo's emotional agony, until his language of passion and violence, love and death, precipitates an improvised attempt to kill himself. The Nurse prevents his desperate suicide bid, and the Friar urges him to accept his lot with patience, to rely on the intercessions of his friends and to think himself lucky to escape with his life. It is arranged that Romeo is to visit Juliet, then make his way out of Verona and to Mantua.

SCENE 4

Inviting comparison with I.2, this scene shows Capulet again discussing with Paris the question of marriage. Again, however, there is a strong sense of contrast between the two parallel scenes, as if the killing of Tybalt has created a cruder, uglier social atmosphere in which conventional courtesies and sensitivities can be suspended. It is also possible that Capulet fears Paris may be frightened off by the social disgrace attendant on the killing of Tybalt. The father whom we saw previously protecting his daughter's interests and declining to use his parental authority over her now reveals himself as a bullying and aggressive patriarch, arranging the marriage without even consulting Juliet herself.

SCENE 5

Contrasting sharply with the mercenary marriage settlement and rough diplomacy of the previous scene, III.5 begins with a lyrical celebration of the beauty and pain of love. In their elegant poetry Romeo and Juliet try to disguise the nature of the world they are condemned to live in, hoping against hope that the call of the lark is really the song of the nightingale. Romeo sets out for Mantua, leaving Juliet at the mercy of her father's social manoeuvrings. When Lady Capulet informs her daughter of the intended marriage with Paris, Juliet of course has to refuse, though she cannot say why. This tacit resistance to her parents' authority incenses Capulet to a violent rage and a tirade of abusive bullying.

Left in helpless subjection to her father's authority, Juliet turns to the Nurse for comfort and support. It is a matter of shock and revulsion to Juliet that the Nurse begins to argue for the merits of Paris, and to discount Romeo as a useless (because absent) article. What the Nurse suggests is, of course, bigamy in the eyes of the law and, to the sensitivities of Juliet, an unthinkable betrayal of her absolute love. The proposal, however well intended, reveals a remarkably crude and utilitarian approach to sexual relations:

> NURSE
> I think you are happy in this second match
> For it excels your first; or if it did not,
> Your first is dead – or 'twere as good he were
> As living here and you no use of him.
>
> (III.5.223–6)

Juliet's apparent submission indicates a breach in their confidence: she will trust the Nurse no longer, resolves to join the Friar and expresses her willingness to kill herself 'If all else fail' (III.5.243).

17

Act IV

SCENE 1

Another link between the play's characters is made through the Friar in this scene, where Paris is shown preparing for his marriage to Juliet. The powerful evocation of unspoken, unsayable truth, which forms the subtext of the characters' conversation, is enhanced when Juliet enters and meets Paris. Paris speaks to her straightforwardly and honourably (as if to demonstrate that, from a certain point of view, the Nurse's recommendation of a socially acceptable marriage was not entirely pointless): she replies to him with riddling evasions.

On Paris's exit Juliet opens her heart to the Friar, and echoes Romeo's suicide threat (using the same implement, a knife). The Friar argues that if she has the courage to kill herself, she will be brave enough to undergo the trials of his own plan to save her and her marriage. She will take a drug that brings on the appearance of death, and so be interred, alive, in her family tomb. Meanwhile the Friar will send a message to Romeo indicating that he may return to rescue her and convey her to Mantua and safety.

SCENE 2

Once again (as in I.2) Capulet is organizing a family party: this time, however, it is in celebration of the wedding he hopes will take place between Juliet and Paris. Juliet returns from Friar Laurence's cell, and simulates obedience to her father's will.

SCENE 3

Having retired with the Nurse to her bedroom, Juliet purports to be preparing for the wedding. Lady Capulet visits her, suggesting a scene of domestic normality. But when the older women depart, Juliet is left alone to anticipate the nightmare of what is to come. Tempted to bring back her mother and Nurse to defer the moment, Juliet none the less determines to face her destiny alone. Carefully and in great detail she considers the possibilities of what may chance: the Friar may have planned to poison her to prevent a criminal marriage, or Romeo may arrive too late, to find her suffocated in the vault, buried alive. Even if everything goes according to plan, the horrific atmosphere of the tomb may unbalance her mind, her life ending in a dreadful nightmare of morbid insanity. She fixes her mind on the object of her desperate passion: 'Romeo, Romeo, Romeo' (IV.3.58), and drinks the potion. The Nurse discovers Juliet apparently dead.

Act V

SCENE 1

Romeo awaits news of Juliet. His servant Balthasar now enters, 'booted' to indicate that he has just completed a journey. He informs Romeo of Juliet's 'death'. Romeo dismisses Balthasar, and announces his intention to 'lie with' Juliet that night. The parallels between marriage and funeral, love and death, sleep and suicide, dream and oblivion now change their configuration. Romeo recalls that 'hereabout' there lives an Apothecary (chemist) from whom he thinks it possible to acquire poison. The Apothecary enters, and Romeo exploits his poverty to acquire a fatal draught.

SCENE 2

Friar Laurence here learns from Friar John that his letter never reached Romeo. The innocent nature of Juliet's 'death' is therefore not known to her husband. Intending to write again to Romeo, Friar Laurence leaves to assist Juliet when she revives.

SCENE 3

Here Paris comes to the tomb to pay his respects to the 'dead' Juliet. He sets his Page as look-out, and begins to conduct his private memorial service. The Page gives warning ('*Page whistles*') that someone is approaching: Paris hides, and we see Romeo enter with Balthasar. Entrusting his suicide note to the servant, Romeo sends him away and begins to open the tomb. Paris comes forward, and challenges Romeo. Romeo warns the other man of his desperate condition, but Paris is determined to arrest him. They fight, and Paris is killed.

Romeo enters the tomb and lies by Juliet. His final speech before he drinks the poison again mingles the vocabularies of love and death, marriage and funeral. The Friar arrives just too late, learning from Balthasar of Romeo's presence. Entering the tomb, he finds the bodies of Paris and Romeo, and Juliet just beginning to wake from her narcotic sleep. Hearing the approach of the city watch, the Friar takes flight. Juliet perceives that Romeo has killed himself, and with her knife joins him in death.

The watchmen appear, followed by the Prince, the Capulets and then the Montagues. The Friar explains the whole story, and his account is corroborated by Balthasar and by Paris's Page. The Prince rebukes the heads of the two families, observing that no one has escaped some measure of punishment. Capulet and Montague exchange expressions of sorrow, and agree to erect statues of the dead lovers in Verona. The

Prince ends the play with a choric speech defining the tragic quality ('never was a story of more woe') of the events in which they have participated, the action the audience has witnessed.

2. Structure and Interpretation

I would now like to shift the focus of our inquiry away from the attempt to describe the dramatic narrative, as objectively as possible, to a more active and engaged effort to interpret its meaning. The obvious point to begin this exploration is with the play's own definition of its moral and ideological pattern. The action of the play is introduced by a 'Chorus', a figure of prescient wisdom like a narrator, who stands both inside and outside the action of the play and is therefore better able to deliver a judgement on the meaning of its dramatized events. The Chorus re-appears briefly at the beginning of Act II but is not otherwise in evidence. Some producers have felt that it would be neater if the Chorus were there to sum up at the end of the play too: Franco Zefirelli's film version takes some lines from the Prince's concluding speech and has them delivered in the voice-over commentary of the Chorus. The voice used, that of Lord Laurence Olivier, is a familiar theatrical voice, reverberant with cultural authority, so in this production the Chorus's interpretation of events is developed into a complete narrative frame, establishing a clear perspective from which we may judge and respond to the dramatic action.

At the play's opening the Chorus lays the basis for the story by outlining the feud between the two great houses, a quarrel rooted in inveterate enmity ('ancient grudge') and now breaking out into reopened hostilities ('new mutiny'). We never learn what the quarrel was about in the first place. The significance of the relationship between Romeo and Juliet is placed firmly by the Chorus within the context of the feud: he calls them 'a pair of star-crossed lovers', lovers doomed to undergo a tragedy written in their stars. The Chorus then makes it clear that this tragedy does, however, entail positive consequences, since the tragic deaths of Romeo and Juliet will bring their parents to a new understanding, will reconcile their deep-rooted familial enmity and pacify their habitual violence. The Chorus stresses this aspect particularly strongly, repeating the claim by emphasizing that nothing else but the deaths of their children could have healed the civil breach: he speaks of

> their parents' rage,
> Which, but their children's end, naught could remove . . .
> (Prologue, 10–11)

The Prologue is in a sense a blueprint for the action of the play, a model in miniature of its artistic and emotional structure. There is the feud, then there are the lovers whose passion transcends it; there is the paradoxical dénouement in which the feuding families destroy the lovers but are then redeemed by the example of their love. There is an element of contradiction in this structure: the love of Romeo and Juliet is the only good thing produced by the feud, yet it must be destroyed if the enemies are to be reconciled. This element may seem disconcerting, even unpalatable, though the quality of contradiction involved in this 'sacrificial' interpretation of the play is regarded as appropriate to some conceptions of tragedy.

As we shall see, however, this contradictory structure, in which the death of the lovers is the price to be paid for the settling of the feud, is a highly problematical aspect of *Romeo and Juliet* that we will have to examine in more detail. Some dramatized versions of the play embrace this interpretation wholeheartedly: Franco Zefirelli ended his screen version by adding to Shakespeare's text a double funeral procession, in which the bodies of Romeo and Juliet are borne through the streets of Verona and into the church. Members of the two families file on either side after the bodies and divide when they reach the camera, separated but joined by their mutual loss. The heads of the families look across at one another, formally but with obvious regret; the Nurse leans across and touches Benvolio, then the servants who follow embrace or clasp hands. At the end of *West Side Story* members of both the rival street gangs help to carry off the dead body of Tony (Romeo), and Maria (Juliet) survives, her bereavement a universal reproach.

On the other hand, some of the play's adapters and producers have clearly been very unhappy about the implications of this 'sacrificial' view of *Romeo and Juliet*. One remarkable production, directed for the Royal Shakespeare Company by Michael Bogdanov in 1986, represents the deaths of the lovers as futile and unnecessary and casts a harshly ironic light on the reconciliation of the two families. Both Montagues and Capulets appeared almost smug and complacent as they unveiled the golden statues of Romeo and Juliet, emblems not so much of their children's sacrifice as of their own wealth and generosity. In order to emphasize this interpretation Bogdanov made a substantial cut in the received text, deleting everything between Juliet's suicide (V.3.170) and the Prince's final speech. Juliet's death was followed immediately by a blackout: after a pause lights went up on the bodies of the lovers, already converted into the statues promised by their fathers at the end of the play-text. The Prince presided over the unveiling of the statues, reading a cut version of the Chorus's Prologue from note cards, while the two families gathered around to pose for photographers. The spectacle of Capulet and Montague shaking hands was presented as a public ceremony, like two politicians at a summit conference. As most of the cast left the stage, the emptiness and hypocrisy of the entire ritual was thrown into perspective by some final additional details: Lady Montague placed a flower at the foot of Romeo's statue, and Benvolio left slowly and in dejection. Both these marginal characters were distinguished, in their genuine sense of loss, from the collective atmosphere of callous indifference and criminal complacency.

The disagreement between these productions centres on what might be called the moral of the story. They agree in taking a positive view of the lovers themselves and in regarding their love as a healthy and therapeutic challenge to the casual hostility and routine violence of a divided society. They agree in taking a negative view both of the feud and of the families who sustain it. Where they differ is in their interpretation of the effect of the sacrificial deaths of the two lovers. Zefirelli's film and *West Side Story* both show a newly awakened sense of remorse growing between the two factions, pointing towards peace and reconciliation. Bogdanov, however, proposes that the families that have callously exploited the innocence, youth and beauty of their children are merely continuing to do so and, if anything, are profiting from, rather than losing by, their deaths.

Although Bogdanov's production was criticized as a distortion of the play, clearly it proposes a possible interpretation of the dramatic text. By the simple theatrical device of using the lovers' own bodies, dressed in gold fabric, to represent the statues Bogdanov stressed a conception already implicit in the Shakespearian text – that there is something meanly commercial, and even competitive, about the final speeches of Capulet and Montague that seems out of keeping with the prevailing tragic emotion.

CAPULET

O brother Montague, give me thy hand.
This is my daughter's jointure, for no more
Can I demand.

MONTAGUE

           But I can give thee more.
For I will raise her statue in pure gold,
That whiles Verona by that name is known,
There shall no figure at such rate be set
As that of true and faithful Juliet.

CAPULET
As rich shall Romeo's by his lady lie,
Poor sacrifices of our enmity!
(V.3.296–304)

Of course, these lines can be interpreted sympathetically, as indicative of a genuine change of heart in the leaders of both the families. We can infer that their strongest shared emotion is a sense of loss and that they are very much aware of the poverty and bitterness of all that is left to them – two old men shaking hands, planning a memorial tribute to their slaughtered children – a poor substitute for the marriage alliance they might have mutually enjoyed.

At the same time we might take a different view. The lovers are envisaged here as transformed from the shameful and piteous reality of their stabbed and poisoned corpses into decorative artistic objects, expressive of both aesthetic and material value. This combined emphasis on wealth and prettiness operates to conceal the brutal and uncomfortable truths that the play has disclosed. Capulet admits that the lovers are 'poor sacrifices', but both families are eager to change them back into something 'rich'. Both Montague and Capulet here speak a language of commercial transaction, sealing a parodic marriage contract in which the principals, being dead, are symbolically eliminated from their parents' financial preoccupations. If Montague does give Capulet his hand (the text does not indicate whether or not this is meant to occur), it may be more in the spirit of a bargain struck than a gesture of amity. Furthermore, the exchange is conducted as a kind of competition ('I can give thee more' ... 'as rich ...'), as if the two houses were still vying with one another for pre-eminence in wealth and status.

There seems to be no acknowledgement at all by the older generation that Romeo and Juliet have been made victims of the families' competitive emulation (the feud, because of which Romeo kills Tybalt) and of their hunger for status and power (the arranged marriage between Juliet and Paris) rather than of some abstract and inexplicable 'enmity'. In a play that continually sets love as a challenging value against the mercenary ethics of profit, competition and property marriage there is surely something odd about the fact that the final reconciliation is formulated in precisely those terms: it seems as if the two families are closing ranks very much in the old way, having expelled the unassimilable element of an inter-family relationship.

By cutting some 140 lines from the play-text Bogdanov laid himself open to the charge of altering the play's intended structure in the interest of clarifying his own directorial interpretation. But if my second analysis of those closing speeches is accepted as a possible reading, then a similar interpretation could be developed from the whole text, without cutting. The basic structure can be open to quite different interpretations.

Other versions of the Romeo and Juliet story offer even more radically dissimilar interpretative perspectives. The primary source of Shakespeare's play was a long narrative poem, *The Tragicall History of Romeus and Juliet* (1562) by Arthur Brooke. This was an English translation of a French version (by François Belleforest) of an Italian romance, *Romeo e Giuiletta* (1554) by Matteo Bandello. At least two other versions of the story, one Italian (Luigi da Porto's *Giuletta e Romeo*, *c.* 1530) and one English (William Painter's 'Rhomeo and Julietta', included in *The Palace of Pleasure,* Vol. II, 1567), are considered possible as source material, so the story was obviously a very popular one before Shakespeare adapted it for the stage. Brooke's translation is preceded by a preface (*To the Reader*) in which the translator offers his evaluation of the story's meaning. It is a very different account from that given by the Chorus in Shakespeare's play.

The good man's example biddeth men to be good, and the evil man's mischief warneth men not to be evil ... And to this end (good Reader) is this tragicall matter written, to describe unto thee a couple of unfortunate lovers, thralling themselves to unhonest desire, neglecting the authority and advice of parents and friends, conferring their principal counsels with drunken gossips, and superstitious friars (the naturally fit instruments of unchastity) attempting all adventures of peril, for the attaining of their wished lust, using auricular confession (the key of whoredom, and treason) for furtherance of their purpose, abusing the honourable name of lawful marriage, to cloak unhappy death.

Here the story is offered as exemplifying a clear uncompromising moral lesson. The reader should consider the fates of these two lovers, obsessed by an illicit passion, rebelling against the legitimate authority of family, Church and state, trusting in immoral and superstitious assistants (the Nurse and the Friar), abusing the sacrament of marriage, and their example should clearly point the way towards the desirability of an honest and temperate life, embracing virtue and shunning vice.

This is not, of course, the way Shakespeare's play is normally read or produced. Yet Brooke's poem is not only a version of the same story – it is Shakespeare's principal source. Is Brooke's preface a possible interpretation of the story? Critics have dealt with this difficulty in various ways: by arguing that Brooke's poem offers a perspective different from his own preface; that the puritanical translator was just using the preface for an opportunistic dig at the Roman Catholics; or that Brooke's poem does indeed construct from the story a simple moral fable, while Shakespeare's play is an infinitely more complex and ambiguous poetic drama. But none of these arguments quite confronts the sharp divergences between this negative view of the lovers as culpable moral delinquents who bring about their own downfall and the more familiar, positive, view of Romeo and Juliet as passionate dissenters within a corrupt and condemned society. Yet some critical interpretations of the play, notably that of W. H. Auden, have indeed taken this negative line, and interpreted the lovers as 'moral exempla of excessive passion' (quoted in *The New Cambridge Shakespeare: Romeo and Juliet*, ed. G. Blakemore Evans, Cambridge: Cambridge University Press, 1984, p. 14).

Not only do different versions of the same story offer different possibilities of interpretation but the same version of the story – for example, Shakespeare's play – is itself susceptible to varying emphases, different readings and divergent interpretations. There are two ways in which the critic may approach this problem. One is to argue for the superiority of one interpretation over another, seeking to demonstrate and prove that a particular critical line fits the play best, or is most in keeping with its historical context, or is most appropriate to its written or theatrical form. The other is to assume that these different readings, being possible interpretations of the text, are in some way contained in it or, at least, potentially implied by it. If we can trace those readings to their origins in the text, we may arrive at a more complex and comprehensive account of the text's poetic and theatrical possibilities.

I would like to draw together some of these threads of inquiry into an extended discussion of one particular section of the play, that in which Juliet is commanded by her parents to marry Paris (III.5.64–204). This could be described as a point at which the play's universality is very much apparent. The key dramatic confrontation is between Juliet, cherishing and concealing her secret marriage to Romeo, and her parents, who have decided to override her inclinations and to force the arranged marriage to Paris. Romeo has been banished for causing the death of Tybalt. As spectators we are in full possession of the whole situation, so we naturally feel for Juliet's predicament. The conflict draws the two generations into a recognizable and familiar confrontation: the young, innocent in their simple need to love, helpless victims of family violence and family authority; the old, ignorant and insensitive, motivated by considerations of family wealth, status and power, forcing their children into loveless unions with conventionally acceptable suitors. Calculated to speak with equal eloquence to the passions of the young and the consciences of the old, this scene seems to exemplify perfectly the play's capacity to appeal to a continually changing historical world that yet retains certain fundamental human problems.

How much scope is there here for diversity of interpretation? Would it be possible, for example, to apply the moralistic critique of Romeo and Juliet as passionate rebels against social order, religious sanctions and legitimate authority? Can we read the scene from the point of view of the older generation, responding with critical disapproval to the lovers and with sympathetic admiration for the anxious solicitude of the parents? Or are we obliged, rather, to view the scene from only one possible perspective, responding to it as an affirmation of love, an uninhibited celebration of the uncompromising idealism of that supreme passion?

I would like to examine this scene in two separate forms, as it appears in the Zefirelli film and as it appears in the Shakespeare text. Zefirelli's film treatment is, in general, an attempt to make the play accessible to a modern audience and, in particular, a youthful audience. The casting of two very young and relatively unknown actors (Olivia Hussey and Leonard Whiting) as the principal characters and the radical cutting of the Elizabethan text to produce an easily intelligible screenplay both testify to Zefirelli's determination to make the play speak directly to young cinema-goers rather than to the established audience of the theatres. The film is an example of a production-text based on a conception of the play as consistently contemporary.

Naturally, then, in the film this scene is interpreted as an uncompromising endorsement of the lovers and an unmistakable critique of the parents. The opening sequence of the scene, which shows the lovers waking and parting, is filmed with great visual beauty and deep emotional intensity, heavily underlined by the romantic musical score. The sequence consists of close-ups of the naked lovers in bed, intercut with shots taken across the bed and towards the window of Juliet's bedroom. The scene is suffused with a delicate dawn light, and our attention is directed from the interior of the room towards the beauty of the world outside. Another sequence follows in which Juliet leads Romeo along the balcony outside her window – the scene of their original vows of love – and Romeo descends into the garden, to leave with a brief 'adieu'. A functional, narrative shot then shows Romeo mounting his horse and leaving the gates of Verona.

For the next sequence we are back in Juliet's bedroom, but now the camera is angled inwards, towards the opposite wall: we are confined in a domestic interior, with no romantic otherworld in view. Juliet's mother and the Nurse stand beside the bed, where Juliet sobs for Romeo. As in most of this film script, the text is cut substantially. From lines 60 to 103 of III.5 the film retains only the following lines of dialogue:

LADY CAPULET

> We will have vengeance for it, fear thou not.
> Then weep no more. I'll send to one in Mantua,
> Where that same banished runagate doth live,
> Shall give him such an unaccustomed dram
> That he shall soon keep Tybalt company.
>
> (III.5.87–91)

Juliet says nothing but simply continues to weep. As we shall see, the play-text at this point is continually associating love and death in a series of images, allusions and dramatic ironies. Obviously the plot itself is linking them firmly together, since we know that the death of Tybalt is the direct cause of Romeo's banishment. But the text goes much further that this, developing imagery that points towards the final reuniting of Tybalt, Juliet and Romeo in the Capulet tomb. Although in the film most of the dialogue that contains this synthesis is cut, its visual imagery of death displays, in its own way, no less beauty and power. Juliet's bed is surrounded by transparent, white gauze curtains. Lady Capulet begins her lines, which speak of the death of Tybalt and the projected murder of Romeo, from behind the curtains, and the same white fabric will cover the supposedly dead Juliet when she is carried to her first (mock) funeral. In the Capulet tomb all the family corpses, including that of Tybalt, will be covered with the same transparent shroud. When, in the final scene, Romeo enters the tomb, he draws the shroud from the sleeping Juliet to kiss her body before administering to himself an 'unaccustomed dram'. Through the subtle and entirely naturalistic repetition of a visual image Zefirelli links the bed of love with the couch of death, the violence of the feud with the violence of the lovers' suicide, the poison of revenge with self-destruction by poisoning.

In this respect the crucial difference between film-text and play-text is that this imagery of love-in-death and death-in-love is predominantly visual and is barely verbalized. Even where it is given verbal form, its impact is often lost through the choice of setting. In the film Lady Capulet's line 'I would the fool were married to her grave' (III.5.140) is spoken to Capulet in a corridor of the house rather than in Juliet's bedroom. The physical imagery of wedding bed/grave is not, at that point, apparent to complement the verbal association. The artistic impression given by this visualization of metaphor is that the contradictory, or ironic, linking of love and violence, passion and death is circumstantial rather than any part of the lovers' own experience. They remain innocent, untouched by the contamination of violence, victims rather than participants among the pervasive imagery of love-in-death, death-in-love.

the play-text it is quite a different matter. Juliet herself speaks a poetic language saturated with these contradictory associations. As Romeo leaves, she defines separation as a kind of death and instinctively, though unwittingly, predicts the eventual outcome of their relationship:

> Methinks I see thee, now thou art so low,
> As one dead in the bottom of a tomb.
>
> (III.5.55–6)

In the sequence between Juliet and her mother there is a strong verbal emphasis on the paradoxical quality of her grief, which is actually directed towards Romeo but seems to be occasioned by the death of Tybalt. Juliet speaks throughout in full awareness of this double perspective, constructing a complex verbal play around the related ideas of death, murder, revenge, love, separation and sex. 'No man doth grieve my heart' like Romeo, Juliet claims, professing a sorrow for Tybalt and a hatred of his murderer.

> LADY CAPULET
> That is because the traitor murderer lives.
> JULIET
> Ay madam, from the reach of these my hands.
> Would none but I might venge my cousin's death! . . .
> . . . O, how my heart abhors
> To hear him named and cannot come to him,
> To wreak the love I bore my cousin
> Upon his body that hath slaughtered him!
>
> (III.5.84–6, 99–102)

Juliet's wordless sobbing in the film contrasts sharply with this sophisticated verbalization of a contradictory synthesis of love and violence, passion and death. The juxtaposition, in lines 101–2, of the idea of a violent assault with the idea of a passionate embrace seems to suggest that Juliet's emotions are deeply coloured by the circumstances.

By the time Capulet enters to harangue his daughter with the crude and violent language of paternalistic authoritarianism each of these two performance-texts has constructed a different perspective on the experience of the lovers themselves. There can be, on the other hand, only one view of Capulet's behaviour. Everything in the text points to a critical response to his patriarchal bullying: his original scruples about Juliet's own opinion, now abandoned; his callous dismissal of Tybalt's death ('Well, we were born to die', III.4.4); his obvious determination not to let the inconvenience of bereavement cause an eligible suitor to slip out of his net.

In this respect the play seems to be operating quite simply to validate the lovers and condemn the father. On the other hand, the play-text, unlike the film, does not quite affirm the lovers as innocent and uncontaminated. Theirs is, after all, a love born of violence and hatred: while Zefirelli's text suggests that passion can transcend the circumstances of its genesis, the play-text indicates that a love engendered by conflict is likely to harbour dangerous tendencies, to conceal beneath its glamorous surface impulses of violent self-destruction, a passion for annihilation and deep lust for death.

We will take these suggestions further when discussing the play's language in Chapter Three. Even on the basis of this simple commentary it should be possible to look again at that 'older generation' of the Capulet family and consider whether or not we, as spectators, are obliged to view them from Juliet's point of view – as a solid conspiracy of callous and insensitive authoritarians trying to impose their corrupt and mercenary values on the passion and innocence of youth. As we have seen, Capulet is a fairly straightforward case: there seems to be little room for debate about how we should judge him. But what of Juliet's mother? Is she not trying to do the best for her daughter on the basis of her own values? Does she not also intercede for Juliet against her father's rage? And what of the Nurse? Her recommendation to Juliet – that she should make the best of a bad job, forget Romeo and marry Paris – however crude and utilitarian it may be, is obviously offered with the best of intentions and out of a conviction that there is no escape from the tightly wound knot of circumstances in which they are all trapped. These three parental figures actually represent different points of view and coalesce into a solid conspiracy only in Juliet's imagination.

The truth of the matter is that Juliet's love no longer has (if it ever had) any social space to occupy. There is simply no means (if there ever was) to integrate the relationship of Romeo and Juliet into the existing social structure. Juliet is bound in a clandestine marriage to the son of her father's enemy, who is now also the murderer of her cousin. If she remains committed to that relationship, she remains estranged from all the structures that give shape to the society to which she belongs. A love so alienated from any possibility of social integration turns quite naturally to desperate passion, to violent self-destruction, to the hopeless remedy of suicide. And that is Juliet's ultimate acknowledgement, delivered at the end of this scene: 'If all else fail, myself have power to die' (III.5.243). An idealistic passion utterly estranged from its society can in the last resort claim only one remedy, boast only one power: the capacity for self-annihilation. 'These violent delights,' as Friar Laurence warned, 'have violent ends' (II.6.9).

I am not suggesting that this type of reading can return us to a simple, moralistic interpretation of the play: we are not left here with an Awful Warning against the perils of unbridled passion. But, in recognizing these aspects of the play, we have seen that it is more complicated than the initial idea of *Romeo and Juliet* as a simple celebration of pure love pitted against the corrupt powers of social division and mercenary morality suggested. Perhaps moralistic readers like Arthur Brooke and W. H. Auden were responding to something in the play-text, something that does not perhaps point towards a moralistic reading quite in the way they proposed but does at least make a romantic interpretation like Zefirelli's, in which love is portrayed as pure and positive, problematical and hard to sustain.

Clearly, then, it is possible to find sharp divergences of interpretation in these dramatized forms of the play – between Zefirelli's conclusion and Bogdanov's or between Zefirelli's interpretation of the lovers and the one we find in the play-text itself. Every performance, every production, of *Romeo and Juliet* is an act of interpretation, more or less liberal in its approach to the text. Some producers feel obliged to accept the received form of text (that is, the agreed scholarly consensus recorded in a modern edition) as the basis for their dramatic interpretations: for example, the BBC/Time-Life Shakespeare series operated a policy of using 'complete', relatively uncut texts. Other producers adopt a much freer approach, using the text largely as a basis for their independent creative activity. Such adaptations are often criticized for their failure to respect the original, but, as we shall see in the next chapter, it can be argued that free adaptation of Elizabethan drama, where the production ends up with a version that is quite different from the printed play-text, is more in keeping with the historical character of Renaissance drama than a production that dutifully follows the received text.

3. Poetry in Performance

In the popular imagination *Romeo and Juliet* signifies various things: an idyll of adolescent passion, a tragedy of star-crossed love, a fable of social discord harmonized by love or one of civil dissension redeemed by sacrifice. Perhaps, above all else, the play is thought of as a supremely 'poetic' drama, with all its well-known catch phrases, domesticated into familiarity by popular usage, expressing the lyric intensity of pure romantic love: 'But soft, what light through yonder window breaks?' (II.2.2), 'O Romeo, Romeo! – wherefore art thou Romeo?' (II.2.33), 'A rose/ By any other word would smell as sweet' (II.2.43–4), 'Parting is such sweet sorrow' (II.2.183).

Many critics have placed this 'poetic' quality at the centre of their discussions of the play, and some have even suggested that the play is fundamentally undramatic, that it is almost a lyric poem translated to the stage. One critical interpretation proposed that the play is structured like an Italian sonnet. The same critic has spoken of the 'artistic triumph' of Shakespeare's originality,

which is in the invention of a means to realize, on the stage, what had hitherto been depicted only in non-dramatic poetry: each lover's intimate and delicate states of consciousness, subtle and potent movements of feeling, intuitions of heart's mysteries. The spectator at a theatrical performance, a public occasion so potentially inimical to intimate response, is here involved in an experience equivalent to that created in the imagination of the solitary reader (Brian Gibbons (ed.), New Arden Shakespeare, *Romeo and Juliet*, London, Methuen, 1989, p. 43).

Here 'non-dramatic poetry' is identified as a purely literary form, designed for solitary reading, an intimate and personal medium through which the isolated individual reader imbibes those delicate intimations of emotional consciousness that can be embodied only in the expressive form and confessional mode of lyric verse.

The fact remains, of course, that the poetry of this play was designed to be performed on a stage in a popular theatre, and it could be argued that its language belongs more properly to that kind of theatre and to that very public environment here described as 'potentially inimical' to the delicacies of private emotional communion. So far we have been thinking of the play as a kind of fictional narrative, appropriately embodied in the sort of modern edited text through which the play is normally mediated to contemporary readers – a book in which the play can be read in the same way as you would read a novel or a long narrative poem. There are many aspects of the play that can be appreciated and understood only in this way, but we are usually aware, when we read it as a narrative poem, that something is missing. We accept that the play is a work of literature: a piece of writing that is still worth deciphering and absorbing. But we also know that it is a work of drama, that it was originally written not to be read but to be spoken by actors on a stage to a live audience and that unless we see (or take part in) the play as a performance, its full potential as an artistic medium cannot be realized: we cannot make full use of it as a cultural resource.

What does it mean to 'read' a play? We can of course read a play-text in exactly the same way as we would read a novel or poem: physically immobilized, concentrating, closed off from other people and the distractions of external space, reading for the pleasures and challenges of narrative, character, imagery, ideas. This is the 'literary-critical' method of reading, and here we are not involved in a play-text but rather converting the play into a kind of novel in which stage directions become physical descriptions; characters cease to be simply voices prefixed by speech headings and become imagined presences; dialogue is no longer heard, as in a stage production, but becomes overheard like the dialogue embedded in the narrative of a novel.

How could this activity of private reading be expanded into a more properly dramatic process? We read a novel to construct an imagined reality: we could read a play-text in the light of an absent performance. That is, we could read the play-text in terms of its performance potentialities, read it as a key to how it might be staged. The reading would not be open to the space of an imagined 'reality', as would the reading of a novel but would be confined within the space of a particular theatre, circumscribed by a particular range of performance conventions and so on. Peter Reynold's influential book *Drama: Text into Performance* (Hamondsworth: Penguin, 1986) proceeds in this way, developing a theory of 'active reading' by which the individual reader can construct, from the clues and directions encoded in the text, an abstract version of an absent performance. This method lies somewhere between literary and dramatic studies: it is in one sense a development of literary criticism, in another sense an acknowledgement that the verbal text requires the fleshing out of a performance before it can be fully realized as a play.

Somewhere between Brian Gibbons's view of the play as a readerly text and my theoretical assertion of the essentially theatrical nature of all drama – between the concept of the text as a dramatic poem and the alternative concept of a text for performance – it should be possible to discuss how the poetry of *Romeo and Juliet* should function in performance. One possible view is that in the theatre, on the stage, formal poetic language functions as a kind of rhetoric: it is the sort of language that is designed to be delivered in a deliberately heightened, artful, stylized way, rather than uttered with passionate conviction; it is a type of language that is self-conscious and self-reflexive rather than direct and naturalistic. Where language like this appears in a production (unless the whole play is written in the same high style, like French classical tragedy) it tends to resist easy incorporation into a naturalistic flow of experience and to call attention to the manner of its speaking as much as to the object of its speech. Poetic language in this context 'foregrounds' (draws attention to) its own artistry, so that the spectator is not so much hearing language, spoken as the natural medium of action, but is rather overhearing language, declaimed as a self-conscious rhetorical performance.

There is at least one kind of poetry in the play that everybody would agree to place in this category: that is, the poetic language Romeo uses to express his love for Rosaline.

> She will not stay the siege of loving terms,
> Nor bide th'encounter of assailing eyes,
> Nor ope her lap to saint-seducing gold.
> O, she is rich in beauty; only poor
> That, when she dies, with beauty dies her store.
>
> (I.1.212–16)

Here the verse is so deliberately formal that it actually resembles the form of a sonnet. Yet this high-flown, overtly poetic language of love coexists with a down-to-earth naturalism, enabling the actor to shift easily between different levels of expression.

> Alas that love, whose view is muffled, still
> Should without eyes see pathways to his will!
> Where shall we dine?
>
> (I.1.171–3)

Romeo is not so lost in his lyrical rhetoric of passion that he forgets the more mundane consideration of his dinner. In the next scene (I.2) we can find a similar juxtaposition of the self-consciously literary style Romeo uses to describe his love for Rosaline with a language of ordinary conversation, as his poetic musings are interrupted by the intervention of the Clown:

BENVOLIO
> Why, Romeo, art thou mad?

ROMEO
> Not mad, but bound more than a madman is;
> Shut up in prison, kept without my food,
> Whipped and tormented, and – Good-e'en, good fellow.
>
> (I.2.54–7)

This coexistence of elevated romantic emotion and everyday social banter suggests that the former can sit quite easily within the context of the latter: it is the very opposite of a challenging, subversive, potentially destructive force. The formal poetry is thrown into relief, and the consequent clash of discourses for a moment makes language the subject of the drama: certainly the language of poetry becomes available to the inspection of the spectator's curiosity.

The lyrical love poetry of *Romeo and Juliet* is not the only linguistic medium to be treated in this way. The play is a drama of action as well as passion: the feud that is its basic structural framework clearly involves a high degree of verbal and physical conflict on the stage. It could easily be assumed that such a theme prescribes an intensity of violent theatrical spectacle, necessarily designed (as in the Zefirelli film) to draw the spectator into an oblivious rapture of excitement. Here language can easily be buried in physical action, and it could appear that when the play erupts into a colourful tumult of verbal and visual violence (in I.1 and again in III.1), the spectator is given little space in which to reflect on the complexities of language. Yet the Elizabethan play-text we have inherited did not permit such obviously theatrical action an unhindered dramatic course. In Act I, Scene 1 the audience witnesses a brawl between the servants of the feuding families, the involvement of Benvolio and his engagement in a struggle with Tybalt and the intervention of the heads of the rival houses. After the mêlée has been interrupted by the Prince the whole sequence of events is carefully and punctiliously retold by Benvolio in what can only be described as an 'action replay'. He tells Montague:

> Here were the servants of your adversary
> And yours, close fighting ere I did approach.
> I drew to part them. In the instant came
> The fiery Tybalt, with his sword prepared . . .
>
> (I.1.106–9)

What purpose could be served by this apparently redundant narration of what has already been seen and heard by the audience? Why should the theatrical spectacle and emotional excitement of the fight suddenly be suspended, giving place to a cool and rational appraisal of its particulars? A tempting solution for the modern director is simply to cut Benvolio's lines here and again at III.1.152–75, where he provides an even longer and more detailed summary of what we already know. The most notorious case of this kind appears at the end of the play, where the Friar (misleadingly prefacing his speech with an assurance that he 'will be brief') spends forty lines (V.3.229–69) retelling the entire plot for the benefit of those who, unlike the audience, do not already know it. Evidently Elizabethan conventions of performance allowed for the possibility of combining an absorbed, oblivious excitement with the detached and rational activity of evaluation. The action of a play could be interrupted for the interpolation of a piece of narration, permitting a character to submit to the audience's reflection and judgement a calm analysis and appraisal of events. The physical language of theatrical action is thus not merely enacted but examined, not only embodied but interrogated.

In common with much Elizabethan drama, *Romeo and Juliet* differs from modern, naturalistic plays in that it is full of a consciousness of its own theatricality; to use modern terms, it is not simply 'drama', it is 'metadrama'. Metadrama is a kind of drama in which theatrical metaphors, references to acting and actors, and allusions to the problems of representation and illusion are so pervasive that they make the play self-conscious of its own character as theatre. When watching such plays, the spectator need not become absorbed into an imaginative world or lost in the lifelike vividness of the representation. Plays that are metadramatic not only present dramatic narratives that show action from 'life', but may also be considered as art and artifice. Metadrama not only represents the elements of a story or dramatic narrative – in this case, the feud of two Veronese families, the precipitate passion of their respective children and their tragic deaths through accident and misunderstanding – but becomes the object of its own representation. Metadrama is self-reflexive, drawing attention to the artifice of its own construction and foregrounding the mechanisms of its production. In the theatre, devices such as those I have been discussing – the coexistence of formal, poetic discourse with colloquial and naturalistic language and the technique of repeating in narrative an event already dramatized in action – are capable of stimulating a complex theatrical awareness.

This multi-consciousness on the part of the audience certainly seems to have been created in the Elizabethan theatre through a combination of very open staging (see below, pp. 54–9) and a much more intimate rapport between actors and audience than is possible in many modern theatres. At the end of Act I, Scene 4 Romeo turns aside from Mercutio's banter to deliver a speech that at first sight appears to be a soliloquy, an overheard self-communion in which the character articulates his psychological experience by talking to himself. That is certainly how the speech is performed in the Zefirelli film. Romeo is left alone in the frame and, in close-up, confides to the camera:

> my mind misgives
> Some consequence, yet hanging in the stars,
> Shall bitterly begin his fearful date
> With this night's revels and expire the term
> Of a despisèd life, closed in my breast,
> By some vile forfeit of untimely death.
>
> (I.4.106–111)

Within the physical conditions of the Elizabethan playhouse it is much more likely that all soliloquy was really an aside to the audience, a kind of colloquy in which the actor would enter into direct relationship with the audience, perhaps momentarily stepping aside from the role he was playing. This technique, much less common in the modern theatre, enables an actor to handle language that is not necessarily a direct expression of the character he is playing. If we read this speech psychologically, we have to ask whether Romeo is gifted here with a preternatural foreknowlege of his eventual fate. If we read it theatrically, however, we can see that Romeo is here performing the role of a chorus, not delivering a private confession but offering an anticipatory narrative that corresponds to Benvolio's 'action replays'. The language replaces the character as the focus of the audience's attention.

The figure of Mercutio is central to this thematic area. Not only is Mercutio himself a skilled performer in the arts of language – conversationalist, wit, stand-up comedian, poet – he also provides, in his curious and elusive 'Queen Mab' speech, a key philosophical statement that directly addresses the complex nature of dramatic discourse, its peculiar dialectic of truth and illusion, reality and fantasy. The 'Queen Mab' speech appears to be the utterance of an unbridled, restless imagination, rioting through dream worlds of fantasy in a covert parody of Romeo's romantic illusions. In fact, Mercutio's unusual combination of the arbitrary fabrications of fantasy with the pointed urbanity of contemporary satire provides an effective illustration of the double-edged power of the dramatic imagination, which can incarnate the illusory, or make the actual unreal. Challenged by Romeo – 'Thou talkest of nothing' –

Mercutio responds with an acute and apposite definition of the theatrical dialectic:

> True. I talk of dreams;
> Which are the children of an idle brain,
> Begot of nothing but vain fantasy;
> Which is as thin of substance as the air,
> And more inconstant than the wind . . .
> (I.4.96–100)

Mercutio does not only talk of dreams: he is actually a part of one, along with Romeo and all the other characters in Shakespeare's strangely persuasive fictional fantasy. Mercutio's definition of his own poetic performance as 'vain fantasy' could apply just as well to the play of *Romeo and Juliet*, which in some ways can be regarded as a fantasy neither more nor less real than the fable of Queen Mab. Mercutio's speech is thus a prototype of drama itself, a fantasy capable of conjuring reality into being. However visionary may be Mercutio's febrile imaginings, they produce a vivid representation, although ironic and estranged, of a real world of courtiers, lawyers, ladies, parsons, soldiers, maids. The play itself shares this capacity for producing, through the operations of fantasy, a vision of the real.

What then is the play's vision of reality? The action is set in an Italian city-state, which represented the most modern type of commercial society available to the contemplation of Shakespeare's historical imagination. Like the Venetian commercial city-state of *Othello* and *The Merchant of Venice*, Verona is an image of a modern, commercialized, bourgeois society. In keeping with all such images, Shakespeare presents Verona as a society riven by a deep structural contradiction, symbolized by the competitive vendetta between the houses of Capulet and Montague. This rivalry is not an arbitrary or temporary accident in the otherwise serene progress of Italian city life but a constitutive principle or basis of Veronese society. Just as economic competition and political struggle provide the dynamic energies or a capitalist economy, so feud and rivalry provide the families with satisfying self-images of dignity, status and power, patterns of marriage and property distribution and a lively social life for the diversion of hot-blooded young gallants. At the centre of this society stand two characters representing the principles of peace and reconciliation, the Prince and the Friar, Church and state, civic order and religious discipline. Each proves ultimately impotent to heal the breaches within the social and communal fabric of Verona.

Some social scientists, notably Karl Marx, have argued that just as this kind of competitive commercial society specializes in producing and selling things, objects, commodities, so in its cultural formation it also produces a tendency for everything to become converted into objects, even human beings and their relationships with one another. It seems unlikely that a sixteenth-century dramatist could have shared ideas with nineteenth-century sociologists, but it is certainly true that in the world of *Romeo and Juliet* there is a marked tendency for people to turn themselves and each other into objects or functions. This is so from the very beginning of the play, when the Capulet servants define the Montague men as stereotypical enemies and the Montague women as stereotypical victims (I.1.10–25). Mercutio too shows that he can regard women only as rarefied, idealized objects of worship or as degraded objects of masculine lust (II.4.39–43). Lady Capulet recommends Paris to Juliet by defining him as a physical object, a 'book': 'This precious book of love, this unbound lover' (I.3.88). This image expresses the nature of conventional courtship and marriage in this society, linking as it does superficial beauty and conventional sentiment, aesthetic and monetary wealth. The 'golden story' of a happy conventional marriage is appropriately 'bound' within a book, suggesting the constraint and confinement of an oppressive social form. In fact, of course, the play in which this image of the book occurs is telling that same 'golden story' – a story that ends with the dead lovers transformed into gold statues – rather differently, and this image clearly suggests a way of distinguishing the 'closed' narrative of a book from the 'open' dramatic possibilities of a play.

Just as Lady Capulet tries to construct the relationship between Juliet and Paris as an idealized object, so her husband indicates in his very different language that he regards his daughter as an object too, a 'baggage' who will have to be dragged to her wedding on a hurdle if she refuses to go there of her own accord. Finally, it is when the Nurse, Juliet's confidante, reveals (or professes) her belief in an utterly impersonal ethic of commodity, in which one man is judged superior to another only in terms of their relative utility, that Juliet resolves to challenge death and to 'make the bridal bed. In that dim monument where Tybalt lies' (III.5.201–2). The Nurse advises Juliet to forget Romeo and marry Paris:

> Beshrew my very heart
> I think you are happy in this second match,
> For it excels your first; or if it did not,
> Your first is dead – or 'twere as good he were
> As living here and you no use of him.

> (III.5.222–6)

The criterion of human value, the axis of human relationship, is 'use'. This utilitarian common sense, masking as it does an exploitative reduction of human relationship to mere economic or biological function, is what Juliet revolts against. Faced with the apparent surrender of her confidante to bourgeois morality, Juliet joyfully embraces a vision of death, preferring the perils and horrors of the Friar's plan to a world of reciprocal exploitation.

We can return now to a central critical problem of the play, already discussed (see above, Chapter Two, pp. 21–6): that is, whether the moral fable of the play endorses a 'sacrificial' view of the lovers' deaths as the necessary price to be paid for the reconciliation of their families. For, as I suggested in that earlier discussion this interpretation of the play's structure entails the idea that the love of Romeo and Juliet is offered as a viable alternative to the civil war of Veronese society. This theory naturally presupposes that their love is dramatized as a force of great beauty and power, an unquestionably positive value in a self-divided world. Thus, in most criticism of the play, we find the notion that Romeo develops from the self-consciously affected Petrarchan lover of the opening scenes to an achieved maturity of feeling and purpose in his passion for Juliet.

As we have seen, the poetry that articulates Romeo's love for Rosaline is a self-reflexive type of language, intended as rhetorical performance or even parody. This studiously artificial form of verse, which adapts the conventional language and even the forms of love poetry, exhibits to the spectator a discourse that it would be hard to see as the articulation of psychological experience. But then the poetry in which Romeo expresses his love for Juliet is traditionally held to be dramatic verse of a different order. Here, it is argued, we encounter poetry of a much more concrete and substantial kind, which clearly expresses a genuine (as opposed to an assumed) emotion, a true (as opposed to an artificial) passion, love rather than infatuation, a grasp of reality rather than an abstract tissue of fantasies.

ROMEO

    O, she doth teach the torches to burn bright!
    It seems she hangs upon the cheek of night
    As a rich jewel in an Ethiop's ear –
    Beauty too rich for use, for earth too dear!
                (I.5.44–7)

Clearly the formality is still there, in diction, metre and rhythm, as are the idealizations of courtly sentiment: 'too rich for use', but, at the same time, the sharp precision and concrete definition of the images through which Romeo apprehends and articulates his vision of Juliet may certainly be regarded as an improvement on the vacuous verse of his earlier passion.

This contrast is, however, more apparent on the page than on the stage. In its dramatic context this poetry may be made to sound more genuine and immediate than the earlier artificial verse, but that is not the same thing as a radical distinction between Rosaline-poetry and Juliet-poetry. Romeo's romantic and poetic idealization of Juliet still expresses a refinement of artifice more akin to the delivery of rhetoric than to the expression of personal emotion. In a critical discussion we can separate this poetry as I have done here, examining it in isolation. The medium of film can do the same thing through the techniques of close-up and shallow focus: in both the Zefirelli film and *West Side Story* the lovers are visually isolated at this point from their surroundings, enclosed in a world of their own. But in stage performance this poetry is only one of many languages and dramatic tones interacting across the stage in a continual play of different discourses. If we look at the whole scene in the Elizabethan play-text, we will find it constructed from a series of rapid and abrupt shifts in tone, pace, style and atmosphere, typical of this play's theatrical rhythm and of the medium of performance on an Elizabethan stage. Romeo's lofty and impassioned eloquence occurs between the fussy banalities of Capulet and the angry intervention of Tybalt. Taken as a whole, the scene is a montage of related but separate episodes – a piece of situation comedy, followed by a piece of romantic melodrama, followed by a piece of naturalistic action – rather than a seamless flow of events in an integrated dramatic unity. Romeo's poetry is thus singled out, isolated and estranged by episodic juxtaposition with other, contrasting, discourses.

What has been called the 'pure poetry' of the lovers' discourse is certainly there in the play, but the kind of theatrical analysis we are conducting may well give it a value different from that awarded by a more literary-critical approach, more concerned with the words on the page than with verbal and physical action on stage or screen. One critic argues that the juxtaposition of this 'pure poetry' with other contrasting languages, such as those of Mercutio and the Nurse, has the effect of highlighting the poetic and persuading the reader into rapturous and uncritical assent (Robert Penn Warren, 'Pure and Impure Poetry', *Kenyon Review*, 5, 1943). This seems a plausible view. Think, for example, of the famous balcony scene, isolated in our cultural memory, where it stands not only as the definitive icon of this play but as a classic

Shakespearian image: indeed, it is depicted on the British £20 note. But how isolated is this scene within the drama itself, enacted on the bare stage for which it was written? The seductive beauty of Romeo's love-poetry – 'But soft! What light through yonder window breaks?' (II.2.2) – is actually juxtaposed closely against the immediately contiguous context of Mercutio's filthy sexual innuendo: 'O, Romeo, that she were, O that she were/ An open-arse and thou a poppering pear!' (II.1.37–8), despite Romeo's perfunctory dismissal: 'He jests at scars that never felt a wound' (II.2.1).

However rarefied and transcendent their language of love, Romeo and Juliet are firmly trapped in the contradictions of a divided society. They attempt, and through them the Friar attempts, to produce a new quality of experience, a new ethic of reciprocal affection that will challenge and reconcile the conflicts of their community. Yet the language in which their experience and ethic are articulated is never free from the determinants of that society. At the same time their relationship can never be fully integrated into Verona's social context. The lovers marry and thereby colonize a space that is in both private and public realms (since marriage is the domain of interpersonal relationships and a general social institution), regenerating both realms with peace and loving harmony. But the marriage is covert and clandestine, taking place, as it does, on the marginal terrain of the Friar's cell – a landscape of romance – and its effectiveness as a social contract is never acknowledged, and its potential to heal is thrown into jeopardy by the projected marriage with Paris that can be neither accepted nor resisted. The lovers' poetry becomes progressively alienated from their social world, increasingly embracing a romanticism that entails not only a denial of society but also a refusal to acknowledge the laws of the natural world:

> JULIET
> Wilt thou be gone? It is not yet near day.
> It was the nightingale, and not the lark
> That pierced the fearful hollow of thine ear . . .
> ROMEO
> It was the lark, the herald of the morn;
> No nightingale . . .
> JULIET
> Yond light is not daylight; I know it, I . . .
> ROMEO
> I am content, so thou wilt have it so.
>
> (III.5.1–18)

Here the lovers have lost their capacity to negotiate the complexities and contradictions of their world in language: instead they conspire to fabricate and inhabit an alternative world of poetry in which the real world is reshaped by private fantasy. This poetic mystification of the real is quite different from the fantastic realism of Mercutio's 'Queen Mab' speech and, of course, is not representative of the dramatic poetry of the play itself. Both Mercutio and the play itself operate by estranging the real world in a new context of perception: here, conversely, Romeo and Juliet seek to deny its existence. James L. Calderwood writes:

Language, as it operates in the wide world, may be less pure than the lovers would wish, but it stands for a view of reality that neither lover nor poet can safely ignore. Time, light, larks, and the usual terms for them remain intransigently themselves, answerable to their public definitions. The lover who withdraws entirely from the world into an artistic domain of feeling must pay for his pleasure with his life . . . (*Shakespearean Metadrama*, University of Minnesota Press, Minneapolis, 1971, p. 100).

Whatever ambitious hopes there may have once been for such a poetry to transform the nature of society, its increasing disengagement from the reality of Veronese society robs it of subversive or transgressive power. Divorced from participation in social relationships the lovers' poetry begins to take on the seductive glamour of aestheticism and the sinister, self-destructive beauty of decadent romance. The perfection of love can be sustained only by a fantasy of utter self-annihilation. Denied any purchase on the complexities of reality, romantic love turns to that most romantic of desires, that promise of union with what is absolutely other, that material equivalent of spiritual immortality: love of the dead, love of death itself. Hearing of Juliet's supposed death, Romeo immediately, and with decisive resolution, prepares to seek a deathly union in the Gothic charnel-house of the Capulet monument. Juliet endures a simulated death under the Friar's drugs and, on awakening, unhesitatingly embraces death, together with her lover's corpse. The 'fearful passage of their death-marked love' (Prologue, 9) is a culmination of that process of abstraction, refinement and idealization through which a subversive energy is transformed into a paradoxical ratification of existing family and state power.

Friar Laurence hoped that marriage between Capulet and Montague would prove to be an efficient antidote to the venom of feud: a symbolic gesture of concord and mutual affection that would have power to negate the antagonisms and contradictions of internecine struggle. His aspiration was, in other words, to plan the outcome of events so as to produce a romantic, rather than a tragic, pattern. Despite his efforts the feud destroys both lovers. But their sacrifice, according to the orthodox reading of the play, leads to a harmonious civil reconciliation. The lovers pacify Verona at the cost of their own annihilation, and at the conclusion become monumental effigies of reconciling and redeeming love.

Although, broadly speaking, critics writing on *Romeo and Juliet* agree in accepting this interpretation, within that consensus lie many unresolved problems. Critics have often argued, for example, about whether the play is a tragedy of character (in which the lovers themselves contribute materially, by their own actions, to the tragic outcome) or a tragedy of circumstances (in which they are little more than passive victims of a tragic process). Sometimes critics have felt that there is insufficient depth of characterization in the portrayal of the lovers for the weight of the play's positive values to be borne on their slight and youthful shoulders. It has been suggested that the lovers never become sufficiently integrated into society to effect any significant transformation of its values. Finally, in critical readings there is often a basic uncertainty about whether the play communicates an aesthetic pleasure in the fulfilment of a tragic myth or arouses an uneasy dismay about the thwarting of young lives.

Although such critical debates usually conclude that the play secures a 'tragic balance' between these incompatible impulses and ideas, there is obviously a certain instability in the critical tradition. While that instability is, in a way, a genuine response to the nature of the play, it is symptomatic of impulsive emotional and ideological reactions to some of the work's internal conflicts, rather than of a comprehensive critical assessment of its self-contradictory totality. The advantage of my approach, which recognizes the play as a medium of performance characterized by qualities of metadrama, self-reflexiveness and 'alienation', is that we can acknowledge the play's ambivalence without proclaiming it incoherent. Earlier I suggested that the play can be regarded as analogous to Mercutio's 'Queen Mab' speech in that both have a fantastic vision of reality that simultaneously represents the world and subversively exposes the means by which reality is represented in art. In this sort of drama the consolatory myths and reassuring ideologies that make up so much of our culture – such as the romance idea that social conflict can be resolved by romantic love or the ideological conviction that a divided society could be united by tragic sacrifice – are not simply transmitted to the spectator in their entirety but are continually questioned, interrogated, subverted and transgressed. As we shall see in the next chapter, when this type of drama was performed under the practical conditions of Elizabethan staging it was naturally self-reflexive and metadramatic – it was a drama of 'alienation-effect'. In such drama everything, however strongly charged with emotional power, is available for inspection, consideration, reflection and judgement. The bliss and anguish of adolescent love, the passionate ecstasy of romantic self-immolation, the cathartic purgation of tragic sacrifice and the reassuring ideology of social reconciliation all pass under the rational contemplation of a vigilant and alert curiosity that may observe and analyse the results of a theatrical experiment.

4. Text and Performance

Go into any bookshop and you will see at a glance that there is an immense number of different editions of Shakespeare's plays available on the market. What almost all of them have in common, despite variations of editorial approach and critical apparatus, is an identical text. As we shall see, this was not at all the case with the original Elizabethan texts, which could often vary quite remarkably. In addition, the fixed, finalized, uniform text in a modern edition is held firmly in place by a critical and scholarly framework of introduction, explanatory notes, appendices, so that the text of the play seems to have become permanent and unchanging.

Consider, for example, the edition recommended for use with this critical study, the New Penguin Shakespeare. We think of an edition like this as readily accessible, since (unlike more specialized editions such as the New Arden, New Cambridge or Oxford Shakespeares) it is not encumbered with annotations and editorial intrusions. The words of the play stand clearly on their own, occupying the whole page rather than sharing it with detailed explanations and scholarly footnotes. But that sort of clean modern text, with its standarized version of the playscript, its similarity to other modern editions and its unobtrusive notes, is actually very far removed from the theatrical origins of the Elizabethan dramatic text. It is the product of a long process of editorial interpretation that started at least as long ago as the eighteenth century, perhaps even earlier. For the scholarly editors of the eighteenth century the plays were pieces of a remote history that had to be interpreted, explained and reconstructed for the benefit of modern readers. Valuable and necessary as that process may be, it eventually produces a play in a form that is significantly different from those it inhabited in the historical moment of its original production. The neatness and readability of the accessible modern text actually operate to conceal the complex process by which an Elizabethan dramatic script has been transformed into a modern literary book.

To regain a sense of what Shakespeare's play was like before this history of editing and interpretation began to mediate the play to readers and audiences it is necessary to look at the play, both as text and performance, in its original context of production. We will look first of all at some facts about the theatre for which Shakespeare wrote his plays and then, in Chapter Five, examine the physical space of that theatre itself as the original context of *Romeo and Juliet*.

We are so accustomed to knowing these plays as books that it requires some imaginative effort to realize that they were very much pieces of theatre before they became works of literature. Shakespeare and the other dramatists of the time wrote for the stage, not for publication: plays were written for, and became the property of, a particular acting company and were initially regarded, in law and by social convention, not as the personal property of the author but rather as the property of the acting company that commissioned or bought them from him. Playwrights could be under contract to an acting company to deliver a certain number of plays a year. In Elizabethan London at any one time several prestigious acting companies would be competing for custom and eager to secure new writing to attract audiences. So theatre writers were very much in demand and could be highly regarded and celebrated, but that does not mean that they were regarded as anything like the sole owners of their own dramatic creations.

There was no law of copyright as there is now: there was a state register of publications in which you could enter a title 'to be staied', thus establishing a claim to it, but in practice this was no protection against the pirates who would steal a play-text by writing it out from memory (or from shorthand transcriptions) and selling it to a publisher. The first text of *Romeo and Juliet*, which was published in 1597, was produced in this way. In 1599 Shakespeare's company issued the second text as a corrected and authoritative version. Since there was no protection from copyright laws, the only way the companies could guard their property against piracy was by restricting its circulation. Once a play was published, cast into permanent form as a book and available on the open market, there was nothing to prevent a rival company from producing it on stage.

Hence the Elizabethan acting companies were extremely reluctant to see their plays pass into print at all. The whole purpose of publication is to render something communicable to larger numbers of people via the trade in printed matter. Authors, publishers and booksellers, naturally, wish to retain their monopoly over that circulation, so copyright laws now exist, in their interests, to forbid unauthorized duplication. To the entrepreneur who ran a theatre, or to the collective of 'sharers' (partners rather than shareholders) who constituted the acting company, the play was commercially viable only in performance: the big money was in theatre audiences, not in expensive printed books. Once the play had exhausted its popularity in the theatre the company would sell the text to a publisher to salvage a few pounds, or a company could be pushed into printing a play by the appearance of an unauthorized pirate edition. The Elizabethan acting companies can be compared with the major film companies of today, which seek to prevent or control the copying and distribution of their productions on videotape.

For these reasons, the nature of an Elizabethan performance-text and of a printed book were radically different. The process by which the plays were written and performed did not involve publication at all: the writer's manuscript was copied by a scribe; that transcript was submitted to the Master of the Revels, the officer of state responsible for approving and censoring plays, and was then used as a basis for a prompt book. Additional (separate) copied were made of each actor's lines and his cues. A theatrical production did not start with a book, with the play cast into the fixed finality of printed form; it started with a manuscript, literally something written, like the typescript of a new play that is circulated among the performers in a modern production. An Elizabethan play-text was not even circulated in its entirety, since each actor had only his own part and cue lines. So even the actors did not possess what we think of as the whole play in a printed or written form. The only person who was deemed to need a complete copy of the play (a scribe's copy of the author's manuscript, or the author's manuscript itself) was the prompter.

Given these conditions, it is not surprising that the play-text seems to have changed and developed along with the production. The variations between the texts that have come down to us reflect the conditions of a theatre in which the essence of drama was not literature, but performance, not a written or printed but an oral medium of communication. The modern literary text, with its emphasis – for perfectly good reasons – on producing the text in a clear, complete, and accessible form, often effaces the marks of its theatrical origin and development. When we look back at the historical origins of these dramatic texts what we see reflects the theatrical conditions under which they were produced and circulated.

Many of Shakespeare's plays, including *Romeo and Juliet*, developing as they did from these conditions of cultural production, have been transmitted to us in separate texts that differ from one another, often quite substantially. In the case of *Romeo and Juliet*, as I have indicated above, the first text to be published was a pirate edition, dated 1597, with a title page describing it as 'An excellent conceited tragedy of Romeo and Juliet, as it hath been often, with great applause, played publicly by the Lord of Hunsdon his servants.' The acting company named there was Shakespeare's. Elizabethan acting companies would not be licensed by the government to perform unless they could claim the patronage of a member of the aristocracy. They were not really the servants of a great lord, being by this time independent commercial companies, but they had to have the legal and formal protection of a peer of the realm. Companies sometimes moved from one aristocrat to another: Shakespeare's company was known as 'Hunsdon's Men' for a brief period between 1596 and 1597, after which they became the 'Lord Chamberlain's Men'.

In 1599 a second text of *Romeo and Juliet* appeared, described on the title page as 'The most excellent and lamentable tragedy of Romeo and Juliet, newly corrected, augmented and amended, as it hath been sundry times publicly acted by the right honourable the Lord Chamberlain his servants.' This text is considerably longer ('augmented' from 2,232 to 3,003 lines). These facts indicate that the first text, the 1597 edition, had been published in an incomplete and incorrect form, presumably without the authority of the company or the dramatist, and that the second edition (1599) was issued directly by the company to put a complete and correct version of the play into circulation. Earlier theories held that the 1597 text was Shakespeare's first draft of the play. Scholars now think that the first text was printed from memory, probably by the actors who played Romeo and Paris, and that the second one was printed from Shakespeare's manuscript. It was this authorized version of the play that went into the first collected edition of Shakespeare's plays, which was published by two theatrical colleagues in 1623. This 1623 edition is known as the 'First Folio', the 1597 and 1599 texts respectively as the 'First Quarto' and the 'Second Quarto' (the descriptive titles refer to the size of the paper used in publication).

If the Second Quarto was a text of the play issued with the approval of the dramatist and/or his company, it is natural for scholars to assume that this represents the most complete and correct version of the play. Modern editions are invariably based on this text and those texts which, like the First Folio, were subsequently derived from it. The First Quarto is regarded as a corrupt and unreliable text; such editions are still generally known as 'Bad Quartos'. Such a categorical distinction is not, however, really tenable. Doubtless, the Second Quarto reflects much more accurately what the dramatist and his company wanted to appear in a printed and published form of the text. On the other hand, the First Quarto, constructed as it was from memories of an actual performance, stands in a more intimate relation to the Elizabethan stage that its 'augmented and amended' successor. The First Quarto represents an

49

acting version of the play. Whether it was a first, hastily prepared script, or a cut-down touring version, and whether it was taken down from an actual performance or hurriedly assembled from an uncompleted author's draft, we will probably never know for sure. What we do know is that it comes closer than the other texts to actual Elizabethan stage practice. The text of the play with which we are familiar may well have been copied from the author's manuscript, but it is not the only version of the play seen by Elizabethan audiences.

Although editors are agreed that the First Quarto, as a corrupt and derivative text, cannot be used as a reliable source of authoritative readings, they also tend to accept that, in terms of the play's original stagings, the first published text can provide valuable information. One area in which editors find the First Quarto helpful is that of stage directions. In Act III, Scene 3, line 108, Romeo – who is on stage with the Nurse and the Friar – threatens to kill himself. There is no stage direction in the Second Quarto to indicate how this moment was handled in the original productions; since it is the Friar who speaks – 'Hold thy desperate hand' (III.3.108) – we would naturally assume that it is he who prevents Romeo's suicide. But in the First Quarto we find an explicit stage direction that gives a different picture: '*He offers to stab himself, and Nurse snatches the dagger away.*' This text gives the Nurse an interjection – '*Nur*: Ah?' – that also helps to flesh out the script into a performance-text.

Exactly how this additional detail entered the text depends on how we view the First Quarto. If the text was an author's early draft, then this instruction to the actors must be a stage *direction* either sprung from the dramatist's own vivid theatrical imagination or devised by the company in rehearsal. If the text is a 'memorial reconstruction', then it is probably not a stage *direction* but rather a description of something that actually happened on the Elizabethan stage. As such, it offers a graphic example of the way in which the Friar, though full of philosophical wisdom and moral advice, cannot respond to a practical emergency as efficiently as the Nurse. There are other examples of the help which the First Quarto can give us: in Act I, Scene 5, the group of Montagues starts to make its exit from the Capulet feast. Capulet tries to detain them:

> Nay, gentlemen, prepare not to be gone.
> We have a trifling foolish banquet towards.
> Is it e'en so? Why then, I thank you all.
> I thank you, honest gentlemen.

> (I.5.121–4)

Without further indications in the text we would naturally assume here that the Montagues simply leave, perhaps in haste and furtively, and that Capulet's remarks are sarcastic. But the First Quarto adds to his speech, after 'banquet towards', a stage direction which clarifies the matter: '*They whisper in his ear.*' This alters the direction of the moment and suggests a much more amicable parting of host and guests. At the same time the question of what they whisper to him is left open, actors and directors being free to supply their own interpretations. Perhaps they tell him they are Montagues and apologize for their appearance at the feast. Capulet, by thanking them for their 'honesty', would then be showing the attitude of compromise and diplomacy he displayed earlier in the scene. Or perhaps their message is a suggestive gesture indicating that they are on their way to some sexual assignation. The stage direction simultaneously offers a graphic physical realization of stage action and opens up possibilities of theatrical interpretation.

At the beginning of Chapter Two I indicated some of the problems involved in that neat and symmetrical summary of the action offered by the Chorus's introductory Prologue. It is perhaps worth mentioning here that the First Quarto has a different version of the Prologue that says nothing about the families being reconciled by the deaths of their children. In the standard version of the text, based on the Second Quarto, the Chorus refers to Romeo and Juliet as 'star-crossed lovers'

> Whose misadventured piteous overthrow
> Doth with their death bury their parents' strife.
> (Prologue, 7–8)

In the Prologue of the First Quarto there is no reference to any pattern of redemption, no guaranteed pattern of consolation:

> From forth the fatal loins of these two foes,
> A pair of star-crost lovers take their life:
> Whose misadventured piteous overthrows,
> Through the continuing of their Fathers strife,
> And death-markt passage of their Parents rage
> Is now the two-hours traffic of our stage.

If the First Quarto is regarded as a copy of the play based on a performance and written down from memory, then perhaps the scribe simply missed a bit here. Even so, it is surely odd to find that in one of the Elizabethan texts of the play the sacrificial motif that we think of as a key element of the play's structure appears to be missing from the Chorus's opening summary.

Critical Studies: Romeo and Juliet

It is my view that the so-called Bad Quartos are actually texts of unique and particular value to us because they reflect the conditions of Elizabethan staging. The idea of their inferiority derives from the kind of judgement that measures texts by literary rather than theatrical criteria. Was Shakespeare the kind of writer who attached great importance and value, as subsequent ages have done, to the specific shape of the products of his pen and who might well have regarded the theatre as a degrading influence on it? Or, given that Shakespeare was not only a playwright but also a theatrical professional, an actor and member of a theatrical co-operative business and a shareholder in the Globe Theatre, is it perhaps likely that he was more interested in the productions of the theatre than the more strictly literary products of a writer's study?

The textual scholarship of Shakespeare's plays is a complex and meticulously detailed science: if you want to know more about it, the Bibliography will guide you. I have drawn these matters to your attention at this point in order to demonstrate that, in its original form, a play like *Romeo and Juliet* could never have had the kind of fixity of structure and form suggested by a modern edition; it was a fluid, constantly changing phenomenon. This feature of the play becomes much more evident when we consider it as a performance-text rather than as a literary or readerly text. In the theatre the text of a play exists primarily as a script, a text for performance. In the Elizabethan theatre these plays obviously existed as a basic structure or score on which a theatrical presentation could be improvised and executed. The dramatic event itself could not have been controlled or corrected by the existence of some authentic text, so the play must, in those conditions, have been much more alterable than we often imagine. Far from being a fixed embodiment of Shakespeare's artistry, in which every word and image occupied its pre-ordained place, the play must have been a changing, developing, malleable entity, constantly shifting in shape and form as the actors experimented, improvised and tested out the play, both in rehearsal and before their audiences.

Shakespeare's theatre was directly or consciously concerned not with the production of literary masterpieces but rather with the production and staging of exciting, entertaining and thought-provoking plays that were thought of primarily as a form of cultural interaction between players and audiences in a theatre. The now revered canon of Shakespeare's writings was in a sense a by-product of his main professional business. It is true that in the course of the period in question a different concept of authorship was emerging in which writing began to be seen as the product of a creative individual: playwrights like Ben Jonson, who claimed for theatrical writing the higher title of poetry, were prominent advocates of this new 'writerly' status. It was in line with this attitude that two of Shakespeare's acting colleagues collected his plays together and published them in the text now known as the First Folio in 1623. That was, however, ten years after Shakespeare's death: there is no evidence at all that he himself was in any way concerned to constitute his plays into this modern form, the totality of the writer's *oeuvre*, whereas Ben Jonson published his own collected plays as *The Workes of Beniamin Jonson* in the year of Shakespeare's death. Shakespeare was, first and foremost, a man of the theatre, and, in my view, it is in the light of that cultural relationship that we should now look at his plays.

5. Elizabethan Stagings

Let us now consider the physical conditions of the theatre in which *Romeo and Juliet* was first performed around 1595. The theatres that began to appear on the outskirts of the City of London from 1576 were modelled on existing places of entertainment such as bear-baiting arenas. The typical Elizabethan public playhouse was a circular, open-air building containing a big platform stage partially covered by a tiled roof. Within a round or polygonal structure the stage occupied a central position. At the rear of the stage stood a flat wall, and behind that was the 'tiring-house' (where the actors 'attired'), which was surmounted by a gallery. Thus the rear of the stage was known as the 'tiring-house façade'. The stage jutted out from the front of the tiring-house where the actors dressed and waited to appear. Exits and entrances were made through two doors in the tiring-house façade: above the doors there was the gallery in which actors could appear aloft. A roof supported on two columns covered half the stage, and above that was the 'hut', which contained any machinery needed for lowering actors or props on to the stage from above.

The audience space consisted of a yard, in which people had to stand, surrounding the stage on three sides, and galleries where seating accommodation was available at a higher price. The audience was thus placed all around the stage on three sides: some stood in the yard around the stage and others sat in the tiered galleries that ran round the inside of the theatre's outer wall. The gallery above the stage may have been used for musicians or for additional spectators; it was also required as an acting area aloft at some points in some plays, but that does not necessarily exclude its occupation by either spectators or musicians. The stage directions in *Romeo and Juliet* calling for action 'aloft' – such as those in the so-called 'balcony scene' – actually read *aloft, as at a window*. This suggests that Juliet may have had the space of a small aperture, rather than an expansive gallery, from which to deliver her lines in II.2. Since in the play-text the actors, when aloft, are not called upon to do anything other than stand still and speak, this limitation of space would not have presented any practical problem.

The physical resources available to the players were thus very simple: a bare, flat stage, two doors for entrances and exits and a playing area aloft. The stage had no movable scenery and no artificial lighting; the visual setting therefore remained virtually the same, except for the use of props, for every production, and the performances were lit by ordinary daylight. As the audience surrounded the stage, the action was perceived from many different points of view, so the carefully calculated visual effects that we are used to seeing in a modern theatre were not really possible. As the productions took place in daylight, the members of the audience would all have been aware of one another's presence; they were not isolated from each other as they are in the darkness of a modern auditorium. The kind of archaeologically reconstructed historical costume we see in many modern performances did not appear on the Elizabethan stage. The theatres used no historical costume at all – this did not become normal in theatres until the nineteenth century – but something closer to what we call contemporary dress embellished with conventional signs to indicate historical or geographical setting.

So the kind of theatre in which *Romeo and Juliet* came into being was very different from a typical theatre today, and, in its first performances on the stages of the Elizabethan theatres, *Romeo and Juliet* was probably very different from the play you might see performed in a contemporary theatre. There are, of course, many types of theatre in existence now – studio theatres, theatres in the round and so forth – but by 'typical' I mean the sort of theatre, based on Victorian models, to be found in London's West End, in most of the major provincial theatres, at the National Theatre or at the Royal Shakespeare Theatre at Stratford-upon-Avon. If your experience of theatregoing is not very wide, think of a cinema: a flat wall with a (curtained) rectangular screen and the audience grouped in seats opposite to it, with the screen brightly illuminated and the auditorium in darkness. The shape of a cinema is based on the Victorian theatre or music-hall, with its rectangular picture-frame stage and proscenium arch, its stage lighting and darkened auditorium and most of the audience (apart from those in the stage boxes) sitting facing the stage. Similar stages are often to be found in school halls, hospitals and other municipal buildings. Some theatres – such as the Royal Shakespeare Theatre at Stratford-upon-Avon – have the proscenium arch removed to create an open stage, but the basic shape remains – the spectator looks through a rectangular frame at an illuminated spectacle.

Many differences become apparent at once. The Elizabethan theatres were open-air buildings, whereas now we expect plays to be performed indoors; many members of the audience would be standing in very close proximity to the stage (something we would expect as spectators at a football match but not at a play); there were no pictorial scenery or stage sets to localize the action in a particular place and time; and the audience would be surrounding the stage on three, possibly four, sides in the manner of a theatre in the round, so the actors had to play in three dimensions, and the separation between stage and audience that we regard as normal did not exist to the same degree.

This kind of theatre made little or no attempt to create the illusion of naturalism on the stage. In many ways the Elizabethan stage was anti-illusionistic. Plays were probably constructed with a specific number of actors in mind and characters included in, or excluded from, a scene according to the number of players available. If you see the same actor playing more than one part, it breaks down any illusion that the actor is the character; rather, the historical characters were 'impersonated' by actors who remained obviously, and all the time, actors. As there was little or no movable scenery, the stage could not represent location. Time and place had to be either signalled by convention, or announced in the script itself ('In fair Verona, where we lay our scene', Prologue, 2), or supplied by the imaginations of the spectators. The physical objects required by plays of this period suggest a basic physical vocabulary of major props – a chair, a throne, a bed – that must have remained on stage throughout, perhaps changing their uses according to the needs of the action, or were carried on and off in full view of the audience.

This need not mean that Elizabethan audiences watched their plays in intellectual detachment, always aware of the fictionality of the drama, never taken in by historical illusion. On the contrary, a performance in an Elizabethan theatre must have been much more exciting and involving than one in a modern theatre. The theatres were, by modern standards, very small (the recent discovery of the foundations of the Rose Theatre in Southwark brings this point home forcibly), and the audiences were tightly packed around the stage. No member of the audience would have been at any great distance from the stage or the action; there were no physical divisions, as there were in later theatres (proscenium arch, orchestra pit, footlights), to cut the audience off from the action.

It goes without saying that the stage of the Renaissance public playhouse, at its most primitive and unfurnished (as represented in the familiar drawing of the Swan Theatre), must have been capable of providing the theatrical resources necessary for producing *Romeo and Juliet* but only on condition that a certain approach to the drama was adopted. The theatre must have been largely or completely non-illusionistic, as no attempt was considered necessary to make the stage look like a real place. Darkness could never be made apparent, as in a modern theatre, so a night scene would have to be defined by dialogue ("tis now near night', IV.2.39), or by a combination of gestures and props (such as the carrying of torches, as in I.5).

A further point is that the acting companies of this period did not perform only in purpose-built theatres. There were still strong traditions of commissioned private entertainment, and actors would be paid to perform at court, in the halls of the nobility or at a citizen's house. The actors of Shakespeare's company may have played at their public play-house in the afternoon and repeated the performance in another place, where they would not have been able to rely on the availability of theatrical devices, in the evening. In addition, the companies continued to tour their plays after they were established in their own purpose-built theatres, taking their productions to many different venues and locations. They would not always have had a 'balcony' from which Juliet could respond to Romeo's expressions of love.

It has been argued that the Elizabethan theatres obliged their audiences to concentrate on the actors above all else. Having little to offer in the way of visual spectacle or special theatrical effects, the theatres relied on the power and vigour of the players themselves. Other writers have suggested that such theatres enforced concentration on the language of the plays, requiring an attentiveness comparable with that of literary textual criticism. The fact that today we find Shakespeare's language intrinsically, and not just historically, difficult induces many people to doubt whether his original audiences – some of whom would have been illiterate – could have understood the plays very well. But it is important to remember that, in a culture that is partially oral, speech has to be capable of embodying all the complexity and sophistication that we now expect to find in writing. Television is a good example of an oral and visual medium with a highly complex language that we know so well we forget that it has to be learned, yet it can be understood by an illiterate person. It is possible that an unlettered Elizabethan playgoer might have been able to apprehend the subtleties and complexities of Shakespeare's verse more easily than we can.

Another view is that the physical emptiness of the theatre demanded an extraordinary degree of imaginative participation on the part of the spectators, who were urged (e.g. by the Chorus in *Henry V*) to visualize realistic settings for themselves. The bare stage was therefore a positive advantage, since it required an active effort of the spectator's imagination rather than the more passive acceptance of elaborate stage spectacle we nowadays take for granted. A different view can be found in the com-ments of Bertolt Brecht, who saw Shakespeare's theatre not as a theatre of illusion but as one of 'alienation', in which the audience would be encouraged not to believe in the reality of what was being represented but rather to retain an awareness of its constructed, theatrical nature:

57

'*A Midsummer Night's Dream* was played in daylight and it was daylight when the ghost in *Hamlet* appeared. What price illusion?' (Brecht, *Messingkauf Dialogues* trans. John Willett, London: Eyre Methuen, 1963, p. 59). For Brecht the absence of 'location' was a positive feature of the Renaissance theatre, since it enabled the drama to maintain a variable distance between representation and reality.

Let us, then, attempt to locate the play-text we have before us into the physical space of this type of theatre. Consider first the question of location. Where do events actually happen in this play? The Elizabethan theatres used a bare stage without scenery, so there was no representation of place, as there often is in modern theatres or in film or television adaptations. At the beginning of I.2 we would naturally assume that Capulet and Paris are conversing in the former's house. The servant doesn't actually go anywhere: Capulet and Paris go out, leaving him alone on stage. When Benvolio and Romeo appear and meet him it becomes obvious that this certainly cannot be Capulet's house. When in the eighteenth century scholars began to edit Elizabethan play-texts, editors would often supply a location: Edward Capell, for example, publishing an edition of the plays in 1768, got around this difficulty by prescribing 'Verona, a street' as the location of the whole scene, and many subsequent editions followed suit. This provides a natural enough place in which Romeo and Benvolio can meet the Clown, but it seems correspondingly awkward to assume that Capulet should discuss his daughter's marriage with a distinguished suitor in the street too!

In the Elizabethan theatres this did not present a problem at all. Since the stage did not represent any particular place, it could be imagined as representing any place necessary or convenient for the scene. An Elizabethan audience would have been quite happy to think of the earlier part of the scene taking place in Capulet's house and then to assume that the location had changed to a street before the Clown meets Romeo and Benvolio. Simply by walking across the stage the Clown could suggest a change of location.

Later, in Act I, Scene 4, Romeo, Mercutio and their companions talk about gatecrashing Capulet's feast. They are carrying torches, partly to indicate that the scene is set at night. The Elizabethan texts show that at the end of their conversation they do not leave the stage to undertake the journey to the feast; they perform instead a pantomimic trip around the stage to the Capulet house; and the Capulet servants simultaneously bring on the properties of the feast: '*They march about the stage; and Servingmen come forth with napkins.*' When the Capulets enter the stage direction makes it clear that the disguised Montagues stay where they are and the Capulets come forward to greet them: '*Enter Capulet, his wife, Juliet, Tybalt, Nurse, and all the guests and gentlewomen to the maskers.*' The Montagues stay where they are, the Capulet servants bring in the feast, the family and other guests arrive by entering the stage area – the Montagues do not go to the feast, the feast comes to them. In an Elizabethan performance, in other words, the revellers would simply walk around the stage to indicate that they were going somewhere – i.e., walking to, and entering, Capulet's house. Again, eighteenth-century editors would substitute for the original stage directions an *Exeunt*, clearing the stage so that the Capulet feast could be staged by a re-setting of the scene, moving the location into Capulet's house. More modern editions, like the New Penguin Shakespeare text, go back to the original texts, use their stage directions and prescribe no fixed locations for individual scenes.

We are today accustomed to dramatic media such as television and film, which represent locations directly and unmistakably by filming their physical equivalents – a city, a domestic interior, a forest, a seashore. The editors of the eighteenth and nineteenth centuries, who laid the basis for our modern Shakespeare texts, were accustomed to a theatre in which location was established by the use of pictorial scenery and maintained by frequent and elaborate scene changes. Hence eighteenth- and nineteenth-century texts prescribe different locations and imply theatrical scene changes within their construction of the dramatic narrative.

Let us look, for example, at the last 'movement' of the play, which begins with Juliet taking the poison (in IV.3). In an Elizabethan theatre in or around the 1590s the stage would not have changed its appearance at all throughout this sequence of events. That, of course, was standard practice and nothing unusual. What makes this sequence particularly remarkable is the fact that Juliet's drugged and unconscious body was obviously intended to remain on stage throughout the rest of the play. The location of the performance changes to somewhere else in the Capulet house (IV.4), back to Juliet's bedroom (IV.5), to Romeo in Mantua (V.1), to Friar Laurence's cell (V.2), to the Capulet monument (V.3). But in Elizabethan stagings Juliet clearly remained on stage: at the end of IV.3, where the Second Quarto text gives no stage direction and the Folio gives *Exit* (a direction that would, if followed, commit the actress to a clumsy stagger off stage), the First Quarto states precisely: '*She falls upon her bed, within the curtains.*'

Precisely where on the stage she would have rested requires further discussion and comment. Much scholarly discussion of the staging of

Elizabethan plays has been based on the assumption that the theatres had, in addition to the resources detailed above (see pp. 54–6), an inner stage or 'discovery space' at the back of the platform stage, recessed into the tiring-house, which could have been closed off from the main stage by curtains. Such an additional space would make the above sequence of scenes relatively easy to organize: Juliet would disappear from view of the audience by falling through the curtains on to a 'bed' inside the recessed inner stage. Subsequent scenes such as IV.4 could then have been played with those curtains closed and Juliet completely hidden. The Nurse would have 'discovered' her sleeping (apparently dead) form by drawing back the curtains. Closing the curtains again would leave the stage clear for V.1 and V.2, and in V.3 they could be drawn apart again to symbolize the opening of the Capulet tomb.

My view is that there was no such inner stage, at least in the theatre where *Romeo and Juliet* was originally performed. Without an inner stage Juliet's bed would have had to be, and to remain, on the main stage and scenes like IV.4, V.1 and V.2 played under the conventional pretence that the characters on stage were unaware of the heroine lying there, unconscious and partly concealed. The curtains would be curtains around the bed, not stage curtains fencing off a separate acting area. That pattern of staging would require a non-naturalistic method of performance, in which the bed and its occupant could be hidden or brought into view according to the requirements of the dramatic narrative. Even if there was an inner stage, this scene could not have worked naturalistically, since the same physical object would have had to change its significance from one scene to another, beginning as a piece of furniture in a girl's bedroom and ending as a bier in her family's vault. So the physical resources of the stage clearly worked in a symbolic, emblematic way rather than, like the stage technology of later theatres, aiming at a convincing 'realism' of dramatic presentation.

In the New Penguin Shakespeare text of *Romeo and Juliet* the action is divided into scenes as follows:

IV.3 Juliet drinks the potion.

IV.4 Capulets prepare for the wedding.

V.5 Nurse discovers Juliet 'dead'.

V.1 Balthasar tells Romeo of Juliet's 'death'. Romeo buys poison from the Apothecary.

V.2 Friar Laurence meets Friar John and learns of the disastrous miscarriage of the message.

V.3 Paris enters the churchyard. Romeo appears and breaks open the tomb, kills Paris, commits suicide. Juliet wakes, finds Romeo dead, kills herself. The Prince and the two families arrive to find them dead.

Although this text does not fix the scenes in particular locations, it still divides some sequences into separate scenes, even though in fact the normal principle of scene division – that the stage is cleared and other characters enter – does not apply. Most of the original texts – including the Second Quarto and the Folio – have no scene divisions at all. The First Quarto indicates a break between sections of narrative, at the points where later editors made scene divisions, by inserting a row of printer's ornaments between the passages of text. This device would have told the actors where a change of stage personnel occurred, but it did not, of course, carry the same implications as a modern 'change of scene'. Eighteenth-century editors formalized those breaks into scene divisions to accommodate the play to their own type of theatre, where scene shifts would be indicated by the changing of pictorial scenery. Thus in eighteenth-century editions of the play, and in later editions that followed them, you would find these scenes, now separated, set in different locations.

IV.3 *Juliet's Chamber*

IV.4 *A Hall*

IV.4 *SCENE changes to Juliet's chamber.* Juliet *on a bed.*

V.1 *Mantua. A street.*

V.2 *Verona. Friar Laurence's cell.*

V.3 *Verona. A churchyard; in it a tomb belonging to the Capulets*

None of this could have applied to the Elizabethan stage, where locations could not have been fixed in this way. They make sense only for a theatre in which movable scenery supplies location by the visual representation of a particular place. The introductory stage direction for IV.4 actually states that the '*SCENE changes*': in an eighteenth-century theatre this would have involved a painted backcloth being drawn aside to reveal another one. Another eighteenth-century edition has a different direction for this passage: *Ante-room of Juliet's chamber. Door of the Chamber open, and* Juliet *upon her bed.* To produce this effect on stage a theatre would have to be able to construct the appearance of two separate rooms on the stage.

In an eighteenth-century theatre the final scene would have been similarly elaborate. When David Garrick produced *Romeo and Juliet* in the mid-eighteenth century the stage had a large set representing the tomb, with tall double doors, erected in front of a backcloth painted to resemble the churchyard – a night sky, trees, moonlight. The first part of the scene took place before the closed tomb; Romeo broke open the doors and entered the tomb to join Juliet. Later this elaborate staging was extended even further: in a nineteenth-century theatre the initial action in the churchyard and the subsequent action in the tomb were performed on separate sets, with the curtain drawn to cover the scene change. When Henry Irving played Romeo at the Lyceum Theatre in the 1880s these two parts of the scene were enacted in completely different locations: the action before the tomb was played on a churchyard set, which was removed behind the curtain, and the action within the tomb performed on another large stage set, complete with stone walls, vaulted arches and, at the rear of the stage, a staircase leading upwards, flooded with moonlight from the churchyard where the previous scene had taken place. Clearly such devices of staging belong to a theatre very different from the bare, unfurnished open space of the Elizabethan stage, but by the time we get to Irving's production, the stage is obviously trying to emulate the theatrical realism later made possible by the medium of film.

Let us consider how differently this 'movement' of the play is constructed in a modern film version, that of Franco Zefirelli (1968). Film narrative normally operates naturalistically, either by shooting actual locations, or faking them by means of a studio set. *Romeo and Juliet* was filmed over a large number of different locations in Italy, since the director wanted to fill his screen with vivid, naturalistic images of Renaissance society and culture. Here is a summary of the film's treatment of these final scenes, taken from Jack Jorgens's *Shakespeare on Film*, Bloomington: Indiana University Press, 1977, p. 265. The initial number represents a division of the film-text into separate 'scenes', each of which occupies a particular location or studio setting; the number of the filmic 'scene' is followed by the act and scene of Shakespeare's text. Most of the filmic 'scenes' have no corresponding act and scene division, since they have no exact counterpart in Shakespeare's text.

22. (4.3)   *Juliet's room.* Juliet pulls shut the white gauze bedcurtain, drinks the potion.

23.   *Outside Friar Laurence's cell. Morning.* Friar Laurence sends a Brother on a donkey with the letter to Romeo.

24. (4.5)   *Capulet's house.* Birds sing. Nurse's cry pierces the quiet: 'Juliet is dead!' The Capulets rush to find it is so.

25.   *The road to Mantua.* The Brother proceeds slowly.

26. (4.5)   *Capulet's tomb.* Romeo's man watches Juliet's funeral, rides down tree-lined road.

27.   *Road to Mantua.* Romeo's man races past the Brother.

28.   *Mantua.* Romeo's man arrives, tells him Juliet is dead.

29.   *Road to Verona.* Romeo rides past Brother, through sheep.

30. (5.3)   *Verona Churchyard. Night.* Romeo dismisses his man, breaks open the doors of the crypt, passes by rows of rotting corpses to find Juliet. He takes off her shroud, kisses her. Seeing Tybalt's body, he walks to it and asks her forgiveness. He holds Juliet once again, weeps, drinks poison. The Friar arrives too late. As Juliet wakes he hears the Prince's trumpet, urges her to flee, goes out. She finds Romeo, kisses him, weeps, stabs herself.

31. (5.3)   *Verona Square.* Two families united in a funeral procession. Prince angrily: 'All are punished!' Chorus: 'A glooming peace this morning with it brings./ The sun for sorrow will not show his head./ For never was a story of more woe/ Than this of Juliet and her Romeo.' Members of the two families make gestures of reconciliation, pass by leaving shot of castellated tower and walls of Verona.

The most obvious area of innovation in the film treatment is the addition of scenes depicting pieces of action that in the play-text are narrated or only implied. The plot at this point obviously involves an action spread over space and time, with people moving between one place and another. In a narrative medium all this circumstantial detail would, of course, be related: Shakespeare's primary source, Arthur Brooke's *The Tragicall History of Romeus and Juliet* (1562), a long narrative poem, spends almost 1,000 lines describing these concluding events. But in the dramatic text all this narrative detail is severely condensed; we have the Friar's indication that he has a plan at the end of IV.1 and the arrival of Balthasar in Mantua at the beginning of V.1. Apart from these details, the only scene with a purely narrative function that the play seems to have needed is the brief exchange between Friar Laurence and Friar John in V.2. The film, however, supplies a running description of the whole plot by adding six scenes on the road between Verona and Mantua.

It could be argued that the condensed nature of the dramatic text was a matter more of limitation than strength. Since the stage could not show time or place, dramatists simply had to work around the constraints of their medium. The development of film technology enabled the dramatic arts to occupy those dimensions of space and time that were always at the disposal of the narrative forms, such as the epic, the romance and the novel. If Shakespeare had been able, as Zefirelli was, to deploy a dramatic technology capable of representing the delays and over-hasty dashes that precipitate the tragedy, he would surely, we may feel, have welcomed it. But it is worth remembering that *Romeo and Juliet* was written for the theatre of its time and worth considering what dramatic potentialities that relationship between dramatist and medium entailed.

Let us return to Juliet's simulated suicide (IV.3), and relocate the action of the play in the performance space of the Elizabethan public theatre. Juliet withdraws and takes her potion in the midst of the busy bustle and preparation of the Capulet household. Scenes IV.2 and IV.4 are simply one continuous action, with Capulet, his lady and the Nurse making their preparations for the wedding feast. As we have seen, when Juliet takes the drug the stage directions indicate that from this point on in an Elizabethan performance the rest of the play would have been performed continuously, with Juliet never leaving the stage. On drinking the potion, *She falls upon her bed within the curtains.* Her mother and Nurse come on to the stage, though they are not supposed to be in Juliet's bedroom. Capulet and several servants also pass across the stage, while Juliet in her bed remains in full view of the audience. It is only when the Nurse is told to wake her that she moves to the stage bed, discovers Juliet apparently dead and calls the attention of the other characters to the girl's silent presence.

The poetic language of the play persistently draws analogies with the maiden's own bed, the wedding bed she should have occupied and the tomb she occupies in her simulated death. On the Elizabethan stage these were not merely metaphors, since the dramatic action demanded that they be one and the same physical location. When the Friar and Paris enter they insistently link, in a series of choric laments, love and death, sexual union and dying, the marriage bed and the grave. The obvious parallel between analogous rituals, wedding and funeral, evokes a terrible similarity in the midst of grotesque contrast.

When the characters leave, the stage direction indicates that the Nurse should close the curtain round Juliet's bed, which is all the burial Juliet would get on the Elizabethan stage. The tragic atmosphere is then subverted by a comic scene with a group of musicians, whose frivolous joking contrasts sharply with the atmosphere of mourning and bereavement. But then, of course (and this is perhaps the point of the interlude), since Juliet is not truly dead and will soon be reunited with her husband Romeo, the humorous jesting of a wedding feast is perhaps more appropriate to the truth of the situation (which is that, if all goes according to plan, the lovers will shortly be free and reunited) than the sadness of a funeral.

Further analogies between the bed and the grave appear at the beginning of V.1, as Romeo awaits news of Juliet. He has dreamed that Juliet found him dead and revived him with a kiss. The vividness of the dream, and its mythical basis in fairytale (though normally it is the sleeping maiden who is resurrected by the kiss of a man), convince him that it is an accurate augury. The speech is replete with dramatic ironies: in the event it is Juliet who will wake from apparent death, and her kissing of the dead Romeo, designed to drink up any remaining poison, will demonstrate her determination to join him in death.

The Elizabethan stage thrived on this dramatic interplay of contradictions: comedy and tragedy, mirth and funeral, love and death, always had to occupy the same physical space and to coexist in a brief and eventful space of time, 'the two-hours traffic of our stage' (Prologue, 12). Those developments in theatrical and film technologies that enable producers to separate the different elements, placing them further apart by scene changes or film editing, may have added a dimension of realism but may also have detracted from the union of physical and verbal power that this particular dramatic text possessed in its original theatrical context of performance.

6. The Balcony Scene

This concluding chapter is devoted to an extended discussion of one central scene of *Romeo and Juliet*, II.2, in the light of the various theoretical approaches outlined in preceding chapters. I will therefore be discussing this scene in terms of story and structure, text, 'staging' (in both Elizabethan and modern performances) and poetic and theatrical languages.

We tend to think of the famous balcony scene to some extent in isolation from the rest of *Romeo and Juliet*. As a single scene it is probably better known than any other part of the play. When at the beginning of Chapter Three I offered a list of well-known catch phrases from this play's language of poetic romance, they were all derived from this one particular scene (see above, p. 32). Any parody or skit on *Romeo and Juliet*, such as the famous TV sketch featuring the comedian Lenny Henry and the boxer Frank Bruno, will use this scene rather than any other as its raw material. It is, of course, a key moment in the play, appropriately regarded as central to its dramatic action and artistic structure. But beyond that there are certain images, depictions of particular scenes in Shakespeare plays, that have come to represent the play itself in the popular cultural imagination. Hamlet holding Yorick's skull, Macbeth with the dagger, King Lear on the heath – each one has become more than a crucial moment in a dramatic process and has acquired an almost independent life of its own. The play in question is recognized as a cultural signifier through that representative image.

Conventions of visual representation have much to do with this: these images are among those most frequently chosen for theatrical posters, book illustrations and paintings of Shakespearian subjects. Through those conventions such images acquire a function beyond their characterization of a particular play: they are also instantly recognizable as classic Shakespearian icons, standing for a whole field of cultural production. People who do not actually know a play, never having read or seen it, may still recognize it, be able to put a name to it, have some rudimentary idea of its subject matter, through the power of such an image.

An illustration of the balcony scene appears as a detail on the design of the British £20 note, where it accompanies an image of Shakespeare himself. In common with many such representations, this image isolates the scene from the rest of the play. It depicts the characters in Renaissance costume and sets them in a naturalistic Capulet orchard. Juliet stands on a balcony high above Romeo, who looks up at her from the ground level of the garden; the garden is portrayed by the inclusion of trees and other vegetation. The illustration is stylized in such a way that the object of representation could be a stage set or a romantic depiction of a 'real' landscape. Either way, the image presents the classic conventional image of the 'Romeo and Juliet' situation: a Renaissance Italian house, a balcony, a wooded orchard or garden and a young man standing in humble adoration, staring up at the elevated object of his idealized romantic passion.

I will be going on to argue that this isolation of the scene from its contingent and contextual dramatic action, and from some of its possibilities of staging, builds a certain distortion into our reading of it, and I will be arguing that we need to relocate the individual scene in its dramatic context, and the type of theatrical space for which it was originally devised, if we are to appreciate to the full its beauty and meaning. To begin with, let us trace the story and internal structure of this scene, before resituating it in its proper dramatic and theatrical environment.

> ROMEO
>> But soft! What light through yonder window breaks?
>> It is the East, and Juliet is the sun!
>
>> (II.2.2–3)

From his very first line Romeo establishes a context of elevated, elegant love poetry. Juliet is, to his observation, not herself but a heavenly body, the light of sunrise illuminating the world with brightness, dispelling darkness and shadow. The naturalistic situation we are called upon to imagine, that of Juliet opening her chamber window and looking out into the garden, becomes transformed by Romeo's poetry into an image of a dark world suddenly irradiated by transcendent light. This initial conceit then becomes a basis for the narrating of Romeo's own romantic autobiography:

>> Arise, fair sun, and kill the envious moon,
>> Who is already sick and pale with grief
>> That thou her maid art far more fair than she.
>> Be not her maid, since she is envious.
>> Her vestal livery is but sick and green,
>> And none but fools do wear it. Cast it off.
>
>> (II.2.4–9)

The 'moon' here is at one level Rosaline, Romeo's now forgotten love, at another level a symbol of his earlier love as an immature infatuation. The moon herself is 'sick and pale', and those who devote themselves to her worship wear a 'vestal livery' (a uniform denoting their adoration of a virgin goddess). Romeo himself has been 'sick and pale with grief' for love of Rosaline; he too has worn the 'green' (both sick and immature) livery of the chaste divinity, but now he determines to 'cast it off'. The relationship with Rosaline is alluded to here as a chaste one (it did not involve sexual intimacy) but also as an undeveloped, adolescent, virginal infatuation. Romeo will henceforth worship at another shrine.

The imagery of religious adoration, of a pagan rather than a Christian kind, invokes the context of medieval courtly love, that aristocratic cultural game in which the male lover always cast himself as a humble suppliant and the woman as an unattainable object of rarefied and hopeless passion. So Juliet is Romeo's 'lady' as well as his 'love'.

> It is my lady. O, it is my love!
> O that she knew she were!
> She speaks. Yet she says nothing. What of that?
> Her eye discourses. I will answer it.
> I am too bold. 'Tis not to me she speaks.
> Two of the fairest stars in all the heaven,
> Having some business, do entreat her eyes
> To twinkle in their spheres till they return.
> What if her eyes were there, they in her head?
> The brightness of her cheek would shame those stars
> As daylight doth a lamp. Her eyes in heaven
> Would through the airy region stream so bright
> That birds would sing and think it were not night.
> (II.2.10–22)

The elaborate conceit that compares Juliet's eyes with stars (II.15–22) is quite in keeping with this lofty and idealizing romantic sentiment. Like the image of light breaking through a window, the metaphor of the stars relates the poetry directly to the imagined naturalistic situation, the darkened garden, the starry night sky. At the same time such a metaphor was a standard ingredient in the conventional language of courtly love. In Romeo's fantasy Juliet's eyes are disembodied and installed in the firmament as stars, stars of such a sunlike brilliance that they transform the night into day. Pursuing this comparison of Juliet with all things elevated and celestial, Romeo then likens her to an angel (II.2.26) and, in a single conceit, expresses his sense of his own humility and his lady's elevation:

O, speak again, bright angel! – for thou art
As glorious to this night, being o'er my head,
As is a wingèd messenger of heaven
Unto the white-upturnèd wondering eyes
Of mortals that fall back to gaze on him
When he bestrides the lazy, puffing clouds
And sails upon the bosom of the air.

(II.2.26–32)

The human being gazes upwards, his eyes showing their whites, almost comically falling on to his back in order to view the angel, who in turn soars effortlessly through the element. Again this image relates both to the physical situation – Romeo on the ground, Juliet above him on the balcony – and, with its binary division between the high and the low, the spiritual and the physical, the heavenly and the human, to the context of courtly love rhetoric. The space of Romeo's poetry is nothing less than the universe of nature. His characteristic imagery invokes everything celestial, both natural and spiritual – sun, moon, stars, angels – and all things light and lofty, 'airy region', clouds, 'bosom of the air'.

Juliet speaks:

O Romeo, Romeo! – wherefore art thou Romeo?
Deny thy father and refuse thy name.
Or, if thou wilt not, be but sworn my love,
And I'll no longer be a Capulet.

(II.2.33–6)

This is also an expression of love, but it is formulated in language strikingly different from Romeo's. The focus of Juliet's attention is not sun, moon, stars and angels but things much closer to the earth: social relationships and their conventional signifiers – 'father', 'name', 'Capulet'. The basic structure of Romeo's entire speech presupposes an impassable separation between himself and Juliet, which is defined in terms not of the family feud but of the binary oppositions of romantic love poetry. Juliet's language is remarkably practical: she is directly confronting the physical barriers that separate them, reflecting on her desire in its social rather than its cosmological context.

Her sentiments are no less idealizing than those of Romeo, but they are much more firmly rooted in reality. If only, she muses, names and family relationships did not determine the possibilities of an individual life:

'Tis but thy name that is my enemy.
Thou art thyself, though not a Montague.

> What's Montague? It is nor hand nor foot
> Nor arm nor face nor any other part
> Belonging to a man. O, be some other name!
> What's in a name? That which we call a rose
> By any other word would smell as sweet.
> So Romeo would, were he not Romeo called,
> Retain that dear perfection which he owes
> Without that title.
>
> (II.2.38–47)

Through their experience and language of love Romeo and Juliet should be able to transcend the familial antagonisms of the vendetta, encountering one another not as Capulet and Montague but as nameless, relationless human beings meeting on a plane of blissful anonymity.

Once Juliet is aware of Romeo's presence, and the two begin to exchange dialogue, the original distinction between their respective attitudes – Juliet practical and prudent, Romeo almost levitating with rarefied enthusiasm – continues to be sustained.

> JULIET
> Art thou not Romeo, and a Montague?
> ROMEO
> Neither, fair maid, if either thee dislike.
> JULIET
> How camest thou hither, tell me, and wherefore?
> The orchard walls are high and hard to climb,
> And the place death, considering who thou art,
> If any of my kinsmen find thee here.
> ROMEO
> With love's light wings did I o'erperch these walls.
> For stony limits cannot hold love out,
> And what love can do, that dares love attempt.
> Therefore thy kinsmen are no stop to me.
> JULIET
> If they do see thee, they will murder thee.
> ROMEO
> Alack, there lies more peril in thine eye
> Than twenty of their swords!
>
> (II.2.60–72)

By identifying Romeo in terms of his family name, Juliet immediately foregrounds the complex social circumstances that any relationship between them must negotiate. Romeo, however, uses a playful rhetoric of courtly compliment to deny the relevance or reality of such considerations. Juliet's request for information explaining his presence is concrete, detailed, down to earth: how, and wherefore? The practical difficulty of scaling the wall is not beneath her attention, and her mind is fixed very firmly on the risks Romeo endures by penetrating such a perilous place. Juxtaposed against Juliet's sensible pragmatism, Romeo's poetic rhetoric seems almost trivial, vacuous, silly. The overconfidence of such unbridled fantasy leads him to confuse real dangers with the metaphorical perils of courtly love. Given the physical context in which this encounter is imagined as taking place, Juliet's simple statements of fact ('If they do see thee, they will murder thee,' for example) seem to offer a much firmer grip on reality than Romeo's airy hyperbole ('there lies more peril in thine eye/ Than twenty of their swords').

Juliet continues to exercise upon Romeo's romantic rhapsodies the critical attention of a keen intelligence. When Romeo swears by the moon, she points out that since the moon is perpetually changing, it is no fit token of constancy in love. She wants Romeo to swear by nothing but his own 'gracious self'. Since they are met on that plane of anonymity, no appeal to external authority is necessary; their love is either established there, in the lovers' essential selves, or not at all. Furthermore, Juliet is able to express through her language recognition of the dimension of sexual experience, of physical desire, that is quite absent from Romeo's speech.

> ROMEO
>> O, wilt thou leave me so unsatisfied?
>
> JULIET
>> What satisfaction canst thou have tonight?
>
> ROMEO
>> Th'exchange of thy love's faithful vow for mine.
>>> (II.2.125–7)

Juliet attaches to the word 'unsatisfied' a directly sexual connotation quite unintended by Romeo, who is too deeply embedded in the language of courtly love even to approach such grossly physical considerations. But Juliet's love poetry has an undertone of sensual passion that makes it a much more complete expression of desire:

> JULIET
>> I gave thee mine before thou didst request it.
>> And yet I would it were to give again.
>
> ROMEO
>> Wouldst thou withdraw it? For what purpose, love?
>
> JULIET
>> But to be frank and give it thee again.

> And yet I wish but for the thing I have.
> My bounty is as boundless as the sea,
> My love as deep. The more I give to thee,
> The more I have, for both are infinite.
>
> (II.2.128–35)

Gradually the field of reference here moves, following the pun on 'unsatisfied', from abstract romance to concrete sensual passion. Words like 'give' and 'withdraw' begin to suggest sexual intercourse. It is her body that Juliet wishes to 'withdraw' and 'give ... again'; 'the thing I have' is, in a common Elizabethan play on words, both her own vagina and Romeo's penis, in her imagination enfolded within it. The possibilities for giving and receiving in the perfect mutuality of sexual pleasure are 'infinite'.

Juliet's language thus spans a wide range of perception and experience, from pragmatic common sense to refined idealism, from hot sensual passion to clear-sighted planning and organization: she is fixing up their marriage while Romeo is still unsure whether he is dreaming. Even if we examine the balcony scene as an independent, isolated unit, we find it possessed of a complex and internally dialectical structure. The lovers meet in the romance territory of a moonlit garden; the poetic language in which Romeo declares his love is obviously a species of 'pure poetry' offering an idealized image of the world, transformed by fantasy, and Juliet too declares herself possessed of an isolated space in which love as a transcendent passion can hold temporary sway. But at the same time, through the contrast between their respective languages, the garden of romance is recognized as no safe haven but a space of difficulty and danger. The abstract idealism of pure poetry is contrasted, in Juliet's speech, with a complex poetry that links romantic sentiment, sensual passion, prudent wisdom and forceful intelligence, and love between Capulet and Montague is clearly envisioned as an unstable force, pulled in the opposite and antagonistic directions of social integration and other-worldly escapism.

Once we begin to look at the scene in the various contexts I have discussed, it becomes even clearer that internal complexity, the juxtaposition of contrasts, is the characteristic medium of this dramatic structure. In the New Penguin Shakespeare text, for example, the balcony scene (II.2) is separated from the preceding scene, in which Mercutio parodies Romeo's courtly love manners, replacing them with a crude and obscene rhetoric of filthy sexual innuendo, by a scene division. In the first scene Mercutio counters the conventional language of love ('passion', 'lover', 'sigh', 'Venus', 'Cupid') with a rich vocabulary of bawdy indecency,

alluding to female genitals, erections, masturbation and sexual intercourse. As the second scene begins Romeo distances his own emotional
state from Mercutio's cynical sensuality: 'He jests at scars that never
felt a wound' (II.2.1). In the naturalistic setting the text calls on us to
imagine, which we can quite easily envisage when reading the text as a
kind of novel, Romeo is already securely housed behind the wall of
the Capulet orchard, safely transported to the moonlit world of
romance. When we re-examine the original Elizabethan texts, however,
we find that there is no scene division indicated here at all. Romeo
never leaves the stage between his entrance at II.1.15, immediately
following the speech of the Chorus, and his penetration of the Capulet
orchard. On the Elizabethan stage, in the continuous action of a text
unpunctuated by scene changes, there was nothing to prevent these
languages of idealism and cynicism, realism and romance, from interacting across the open stage in a complex relationship of parallelism
and contrast.

In the medium of film, or on a stage with scene changes, these
languages can, of course, be separated by space as well as time. In terms
of naturalistic action perhaps they should be, since Romeo has after all
clambered over the 'high, and hard to climb' walls of Capulet's orchard.
Benvolio even seems to point to such a physical barrier: 'He ran this way
and leapt this orchard wall' (II.1.5). In Zefirelli's film Romeo physically
climbs a high wall, leaving behind him the ribald, drunken shouting of
his companions and entering the completely separate world of the
moonlit garden. The wall encloses both the lovers and their language,
establishing a romantic otherworld protected from the crude language of
the streets.

Of course, this is not so easy to accomplish on stage. An eighteenth-
century editor, Edward Capell, was the first to suggest that the play
might require a wall on the stage to divide it into the separate areas of
the street and Capulet's orchard: he supplied for Romeo the stage
direction 'leaps the wall'. The same text locates the scene in 'An open
Place, adjoining Capulet's garden'. The location instruction in a later
eighteenth-century edition (that of Edmund Malone, 1790) gives some
idea of the elaborate stage sets available to the theatres of the time:
'Capulet's orchard; to the one side the outer wall with a lane beyond, to the
other Capulet's house showing an upper window.' Some scholars have
even suggested, projecting this kind of stage realism on to the Elizabethan
platform stage, that the play may have used a wall in its original
performances. Since, in whatever way the stage may have been divided,
part of the audience would not have been able to see what was going on

at the other side of the wall, this seems, to say the least, improbable. The scene change to be found in all editions since the eighteenth century is not featured in the Elizabethan texts and clearly had no function on the Elizabethan stage. The physical conditions of the Elizabethan playhouse, and the dramatic shape of the Elizabethan play-text, both prescribe a very different theatrical technique: a swiftly alternating montage of separate episodes and differentiated styles, so that 'pure poetry' is always heard in close juxtaposition with other languages. Towards the end of the scene that sense of contradiction is emphasized by the text, when we see Juliet alternately being called by the Nurse (*Nurse calls within*) and lured back into the moonlit garden, back into the rarefied romance world of Romeo's love poetry.

The Zefirelli film, building on the pictorial stage realism practised in the eighteenth-century theatre and recorded in the eighteenth-century editions of Shakespeare, was thus able to produce a performance inter-pretation of the play quite different from anything that could have been produced on the Elizabethan stage. While the former clearly presents an accessible modern Shakespeare, it also simplifies the possibilities of meaning latent in the theatrical text, delivering a more purely romantic *Romeo and Juliet* than the Elizabethan playgoer witnessed around 1595.

Is this observation mere nostalgia for a theatre long since vanished beneath the rubble of time (and very quickly, whenever traces of it surface, buried again by the property developers)? Perhaps so: but the complex capacity for a pluralistic performance still rests within the dramatic text and can still be released by the right combination of historical insight and modern theatrical ingenuity. Think, for example, of a famous scene from *West Side Story* (not the balcony scene, but the equivalent of *Romeo and Juliet*, III.2), in which Tony and Maria, in-dependently anticipating that night's meeting, sing (separately but in unison) 'Tonight, tonight, won't be just any night . . .', while the two rival street gangs, again separated in space but united in music, contribute an aggressive disharmony in their version of the same number: 'We're gonna have a rumble, tonight . . .' Here the musical score in which each separate element has a place provides an artistic space similar to the unified world of the Elizabethan platform stage. The film technique of intercutting enables the four separate parties (Tony, Maria, the Jets and the Sharks) to be juxtaposed on screen, not simultaneously but in rapid sequence, although each is to be imagined as occupying an unrelated physical space. The musical score links these separate elements in a complex but indissoluble unity, an interplay of harmony and discord, precisely parallel to the complex unity of the Elizabethan public stage.

This is just one example of a performance-text that brings us closer to the true dramatic and theatrical nature of *Romeo and Juliet* than many an essay in literary criticism.

Bibliography

Texts

New Penguin Shakespeare *Romeo and Juliet*, edited by T. J. B. Spencer (Harmondsworth: Penguin, 1967).

New Cambridge Shakespeare *Romeo and Juliet*, edited by G. Blakemore Evans (Cambridge: Cambridge University Press, 1984).

Criticism

H. B. Charlton, *Shakespearean Tragedy* (Cambridge: Cambridge University Press, 1948).

Bertrand Evans, *Shakespeare's Tragic Practice* (Oxford: Clarendon Press, 1979).

Barbara Hodgdon, 'Absent Bodies, Present Voices: Performance Work and the Close of Romeo and Juliet's Golden Story', *Theatre Journal*, 4:3 (1989).

Coppelia Kahn, *Man's Estate: Masculine Identity in Shakespeare* (Berkeley: University of California Press, 1981).

Bryan Loughrey and Neil Taylor (editors), *Shakespeare's Early Tragedies: A Casebook* (London: Macmillan, 1990).

M. M. Mahood, 'Wordplay in *Romeo and Juliet*', in *Shakespeare's Tragedies*, edited by Laurence Lerner (Harmondsworth: Penguin, 1963).

Phyllis Rackin, *Shakespeare's Tragedies* (New York: Frederick Ungar, 1978).

Performance

Jack J. Jorgens, *Shakespeare on Film* (Bloomington: Indiana University Press, 1977).

Jill Levenson, *Shakespeare in Performance: 'Romeo and Juliet'* (Manchester: Manchester University Press, 1988).

FOR THE BEST IN PAPERBACKS, LOOK FOR THE 🐧

In every corner of the world, on every subject under the sun, Penguin represents quality and variety – the very best in publishing today.

For complete information about books available from Penguin – including Puffins, Penguin Classics and Arkana – and how to order them, write to us at the appropriate address below. Please note that for copyright reasons the selection of books varies from country to country.

In the United Kingdom: Please write to *Dept E.P., Penguin Books Ltd, Harmondsworth, Middlesex, UB7 0DA.*

If you have any difficulty in obtaining a title, please send your order with the correct money, plus ten per cent for postage and packaging, to *PO Box No 11, West Drayton, Middlesex*

In the United States: Please write to *Dept BA, Penguin, 299 Murray Hill Parkway, East Rutherford, New Jersey 07073*

In Canada: Please write to *Penguin Books Canada Ltd, 2801 John Street, Markham, Ontario L3R 1B4*

In Australia: Please write to the *Marketing Department, Penguin Books Australia Ltd, P.O. Box 257, Ringwood, Victoria 3134*

In New Zealand: Please write to the *Marketing Department, Penguin Books (NZ) Ltd, Private Bag, Takapuna, Auckland 9*

In India: Please write to *Penguin Overseas Ltd, 706 Eros Apartments, 56 Nehru Place, New Delhi, 110019*

In the Netherlands: Please write to *Penguin Books Netherlands B.V., Postbus 195, NL–1380AD Weesp*

In West Germany: Please write to *Penguin Books Ltd, Friedrichstrasse 10–12, D–6000 Frankfurt/Main 1*

In Spain: Please write to *Longman Penguin España, Calle San Nicolas 15, E–28013 Madrid*

In Italy: Please write to *Penguin Italia s.r.l., Via Como 4, I-20096 Pioltello (Milano)*

In France: Please write to *Penguin Books Ltd, 39 Rue de Montmorency, F-75003 Paris*

In Japan: Please write to *Longman Penguin Japan Co Ltd, Yamaguchi Building, 2–12–9 Kanda Jimbocho, Chiyoda-Ku, Tokyo 101*

FOR THE BEST IN PAPERBACKS, LOOK FOR THE 🐧

PENGUIN CLASSICS

Matthew Arnold	**Selected Prose**
Jane Austen	**Emma**
	Lady Susan, The Watsons, Sanditon
	Mansfield Park
	Northanger Abbey
	Persuasion
	Pride and Prejudice
	Sense and Sensibility
Anne Brontë	**Agnes Grey**
	The Tenant of Wildfell Hall
Charlotte Brontë	**Jane Eyre**
	Shirley
	Villette
Emily Brontë	**Wuthering Heights**
Samuel Butler	**Erewhon**
	The Way of All Flesh
Thomas Carlyle	**Selected Writings**
Wilkie Collins	**The Moonstone**
	The Woman in White
Charles Darwin	**The Origin of Species**
	The Voyage of the Beagle
Benjamin Disraeli	**Sybil**
George Eliot	**Adam Bede**
	Daniel Deronda
	Felix Holt
	Middlemarch
	The Mill on the Floss
	Romola
	Scenes of Clerical Life
	Silas Marner
Elizabeth Gaskell	**Cranford and Cousin Phillis**
	The Life of Charlotte Brontë
	Mary Barton
	North and South
	Wives and Daughters

FOR THE BEST IN PAPERBACKS, LOOK FOR THE 🐧

PENGUIN CLASSICS

Charles Dickens	**American Notes for General Circulation**
	Barnaby Rudge
	Bleak House
	The Christmas Books
	David Copperfield
	Dombey and Son
	Great Expectations
	Hard Times
	Little Dorrit
	Martin Chuzzlewit
	The Mystery of Edwin Drood
	Nicholas Nickleby
	The Old Curiosity Shop
	Oliver Twist
	Our Mutual Friend
	The Pickwick Papers
	Selected Short Fiction
	A Tale of Two Cities
Edward Gibbon	**The Decline and Fall of the Roman Empire**
George Gissing	**New Grub Street**
William Godwin	**Caleb Williams**
Edmund Gosse	**Father and Son**
Thomas Hardy	**The Distracted Preacher and Other Tales**
	Far From the Madding Crowd
	Jude the Obscure
	The Mayor of Casterbridge
	The Return of the Native
	Tess of the d'Urbervilles
	The Trumpet Major
	Under the Greenwood Tree
	The Woodlanders

FOR THE BEST IN PAPERBACKS, LOOK FOR THE 🐧

PENGUIN CLASSICS

Richard Jefferies	Landscape with Figures
Thomas Macaulay	The History of England
Henry Mayhew	Selections from London Labour and The London Poor
John Stuart Mill	On Liberty
William Morris	News from Nowhere and Selected Writings and Designs
Walter Pater	Marius the Epicurean
John Ruskin	'Unto This Last' and Other Writings
Sir Walter Scott	Ivanhoe
Robert Louis Stevenson	Dr Jekyll and Mr Hyde
William Makepeace Thackeray	The History of Henry Esmond
	Vanity Fair
Anthony Trollope	Barchester Towers
	Framley Parsonage
	Phineas Finn
	The Warden
Mrs Humphrey Ward	Helbeck of Bannisdale
Mary Wollstonecraft	Vindication of the Rights of Woman
Dorothy and William Wordsworth	Home at Grasmere

FOR THE BEST IN PAPERBACKS, LOOK FOR THE 🐧

PENGUIN PASSNOTES

This comprehensive series, designed to help GCSE students, includes:

SUBJECTS
Biology
Chemistry
Economics
English Language
Geography
Human Biology
Mathematics
Nursing
Oral English
Physics

SHAKESPEARE
As You Like It
Henry IV Part I
Henry V
Julius Caesar
Macbeth
The Merchant of Venice
A Midsummer Night's Dream
Romeo and Juliet
Twelfth Night

LITERATURE
Across the Barricades
The Catcher in the Rye
Cider with Rosie
The Crucible
Death of a Salesman
Far From the Madding Crowd
Great Expectations
Gregory's Girl
I am the Cheese
I'm the King of the Castle
The Importance of Being Earnest
Jane Eyre
Joby
Journey's End
Kes
Lord of the Flies
A Man for All Seasons
The Mayor of Casterbridge
My Family and Other Animals
Oliver Twist
The Pardoner's Tale
Pride and Prejudice
The Prologue to the Canterbury
   Tales
Pygmalion
Roots
The Royal Hunt of the Sun
Silas Marner
A Taste of Honey
To Kill a Mockingbird
Wuthering Heights
Z for Zachariah

FOR THE BEST IN PAPERBACKS, LOOK FOR THE 🐧

PENGUIN MASTERSTUDIES

Masterstudies are the ideal companions to course-work and revision, specially designed for advanced-level students and first-year undergraduates.

Masterstudies are stimulating, thorough and up to date. Each volume takes full account of recent syllabus changes. All are written by experienced teachers with excellent records in examination success.

Whatever your subject, *Masterstudies* will give you a comprehensive overview of the syllabus, enable you to test your examination technique and ensure you are well-prepared to face your exams with confidence.

subjects include:

Biology
Drama: Text into Performance
Economics
Geography
Physics
Pure Mathematics

FOR THE BEST IN PAPERBACKS, LOOK FOR THE

PENGUIN SELF-STARTERS

Self-Starters are designed to help you develop skills and proficiency in the subject of your choice. Each book has been written by an expert and is suitable for school-leavers, students, those considering changing their career in mid-stream and all those who study at home.

Titles published or in preparation:

Accounting	Noel Trimming
Acting	Nigel Rideout
Advertising	Michael Pollard
Basic Statistics	Peter Gwilliam
Business Communication	Doris Wheatley
A Career in Banking	Sheila Black, John Brennan
Clear English	Vivian Summers
Fashion and Design	Ken Baynes, Krysia Brochocka, Beverly Saunders
Five-Hour Keyboarding Course	Madeleine Brearley
Job-Hunting	Alfred Hossack
Marketing	Marsaili Cameron, Angela Rushton, David Carson
Nursing	David White
Personnel Management	J. D. Preston
Public Relations	Sheila Black, John Brennan
Public Speaking	Vivian Summers
Report Writing	Doris Wheatley
Retailing	David Couch
Secretarial Skills	Gail Cornish, Charlotte Coudrille, Joan Lipkin-Edwardes
Starting a Business on a Shoestring	Michel Syrett, Chris Dunn
Typing	Gill Sugden